Building Outstanding Leadership Teams

Insights from charity chief executives

Mike Hudson
Director, Compass Partnership

Jacinta Ashworth
Research Consultant, Compass Partnership

In association with
Centre for Charity Effectiveness, Cass Business School

Published by

Compass Partnership

Greenbanks

New Road

Bourne End

Buckinghamshire

SL8 5BZ

Tel: 01628 478561

Email: demerson@compassnet.co.uk

www.compasspartnership.co.uk

Distributed by

Directory of Social Change

24 Stephenson Way

London

NW1 2DP

Tel: 0845 077 7707

Email: publications@dsc.org.uk

www.dsc.org.uk/bol

from whom further copies are available.

Print ISBN 978 1 906294 93 9

Digital ISBN 978 1 906294 94 6

Contents

The authors

Mike Hudson is the Director of Compass Partnership. He was a Director of Friends of the Earth during its formative years. Following this, he worked in the UK and USA for a business strategy consultancy. He has worked as a consultant to not-for-profit organisations for over 25 years leading teams that bring about change in complex organisations.

His clients include the chairs and chief executives of a wide range of national and international organisations in health, housing, education and international development, and their government and foundation funders. In addition to managing Compass, Mike is currently a Visiting Fellow at Cass Business School in London.

His book, *Managing Without Profit, Leadership, Management and Governance of Third Sector Organisations* (Third Edition, DSC, 2009), has sold 20,000 copies, been translated into three languages and published in an Australian edition. Until recently he was a member of the Board of the Leadership Foundation for Higher Education and Chair of its Audit Committee. He is a member of the Editorial Board of *Civil Society Governance* magazine.

Jacinta Ashworth graduated with first class honours from the University of Bristol and has over 20 years' experience in conducting market and social research. From 1992 to 2001 she was employed by BMRB International, a leading UK market research agency where she managed research for the public and nonprofit sectors, covering health and disability, human resources, crime, citizenship, volunteering, racial discrimination, employment, benefits and international development.

Jacinta's published research includes surveys for the Home Office, the British Heart Foundation, Scope and Tearfund among others.

Since 2003 she has been a Research Consultant with Compass Partnership, conducting governance assignments for the NSPCC, the Royal College of Nursing, the MS Society and Citizens Advice, and carrying out research to inform strategic reviews for the Willow Foundation, DrinkAware and Turn2Us. She has also managed extensive welfare policy research for The Royal British Legion, co-authoring a series of published reports on veterans' needs. She is a trustee of Thames Hospice.

Mike Hudson and Jacinta Ashworth are also joint authors of *Delivering Effective Governance, Insights from the boards of larger charities*, the similar study into the governance of larger charities.

Executive Summary

Charities make a huge contribution to life in the UK. The larger ones are highly complex organisations often working in very challenging situations that place huge demands on their leadership and management. Yet, surprisingly, remarkably little is known about how leadership teams are structured, how stable their membership is, how members work as a team, what they do to invest in their development and how they provide leadership across their organisations.

We set out to answer these questions by investigating the workings of the leadership teams of the UK's larger charities. We did a literature review, held workshops and used our consulting experience to establish a research model[1] that described the key characteristics of leadership teams and that could be used to assess how well they are delivered and what impact they have on leadership team performance.

We then organised these characteristics into nine components of leadership team effectiveness:

THE COMPONENTS OF LEADERSHIP TEAM EFFECTIVENESS

LEADERSHIP TEAM

Organising the team	Managing the team	Leading the organisation
1. Team structure 2. Team membership 3. Team leader 4. Team recruitment and reward	5. Team meetings 6. Team working 7. Team development	8. Leadership of strategy and impact 9. Leadership of behaviour

We used this structure to pilot a survey and then gather detailed information from the chief executives of 102 of the UK's top 500 charities about how teams are organised and managed, how they lead their organisations and how effective chief executives thought their organisations were at performing each of the main components. We checked these findings with a sample of HR directors.

We recognise that effective leadership teams are only one element of creating effective charities and that an effective leadership team might not equate to an effective charity. We also recognise that boards, staff members and other team members might have a very different perspective on the performance of their organisation's leadership team. Despite these limitations, we believe that by dividing leadership team arrangements into their constituent parts, setting out how they work at present and identifying the characteristics that contribute most strongly to high performing teams, we have created a framework for teams to analyse their arrangements, benchmark their performance and pinpoint the improvements that will have the greatest leverage on team effectiveness.

---

[1] The full model is set out in Appendix 6

In summary leadership teams had the following features:

Organising the team

Team structure
- Almost two thirds had a single leadership team, without a core group or wider team
- Most thought their team size was right
- A fifth had a chief operating officer.

Team membership
- The average team had 6.5 members (including the chief executive)
- Overall 44% of team members were female and 85% were white British
- 36% of team members had post graduate qualifications
- Two thirds were external appointments rather than promotions
- Average time in post was 5.2 years, so a typical team changed by one person per year.

Team leader
- One third were women and just over 11% were from an ethnic minority
- Half of the leaders were in their first chief executive role
- Three quarters were external appointments
- On average they had been in post for 6.7 years
- 71% had a position on another board.

Recruitment and reward
- Half of the organisations had used personality tests in recruiting leadership team members
- In four in ten teams, members were eligible for performance related payments
- 82% of organisations offered flexible working arrangements.

Managing the team

Team meetings
- Teams typically spent 15 days per year in all types of leadership team meetings
- In 10% of teams the chief executive didn't chair leadership team meetings
- A third formally reviewed performance of team meetings at least once a year.

Team working
- Three quarters have discussed how they want to work together
- Three fifths have discussed why the team exists
- Half have discussed what they expect of each other.

Team development
- 21% conducted a review of the performance of the team in the last three years
- Four fifths had used external training and nearly a third had a team coach for six months or more
- A third of chief executives had used a personal coach, a third had used a mentor and a quarter had received training in team leadership skills
- Three quarters had taken any action to get a team member to leave in the last three years.

Leading the organisation

Leadership of strategy and impact

- Almost all organisations had some quantified and time bound strategic objectives and in half of organisations most objectives were quantified and time bound
- Teams typically review strategic performance and the risk register quarterly.

Leadership of behaviour across the organisation

- The majority of teams had taken steps to establish values and behaviours across the organisation
- Two thirds actively discouraged silo working
- Only 30% reported that breaches of values were dealt with swiftly and diligently.

We asked chief executives to rate performance on each of the nine components in the model and to rate the overall effectiveness of their leadership team:

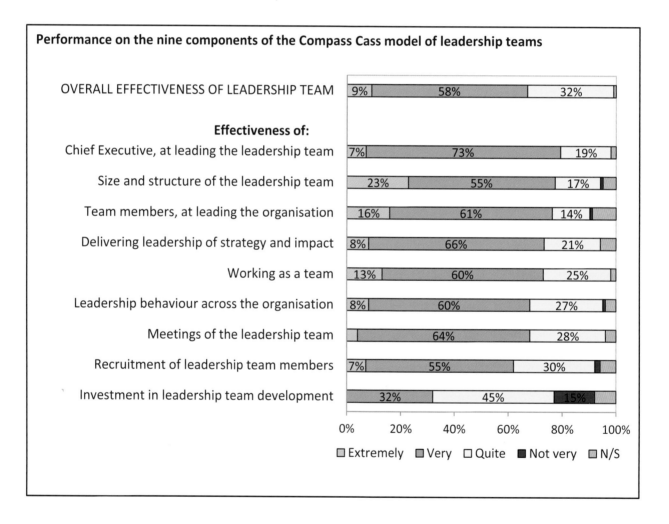

Performance on the nine components of the Compass Cass model of leadership teams

	Extremely	Very	Quite	Not very	N/S
OVERALL EFFECTIVENESS OF LEADERSHIP TEAM	9%	58%	32%		
Effectiveness of:					
Chief Executive, at leading the leadership team	7%	73%	19%		
Size and structure of the leadership team	23%	55%	17%		
Team members, at leading the organisation	16%	61%	14%		
Delivering leadership of strategy and impact	8%	66%	21%		
Working as a team	13%	60%	25%		
Leadership behaviour across the organisation	8%	60%	27%		
Meetings of the leadership team		64%	28%		
Recruitment of leadership team members	7%	55%	30%		
Investment in leadership team development	32%	45%	15%		

We then looked at correlations between the nine components of the team in our model and ratings of overall team performance to identify the 'drivers' of high performing teams. Five components stood out significantly ahead of the others

We went on to identify the underlying characteristics that contribute to each of these, to give leadership teams an indication of what is likely to have the greatest impact on team performance. This led to our model of outstanding leadership team performance:

DRIVERS OF OUTSTANDING LEADERSHIP TEAM PERFORMANCE

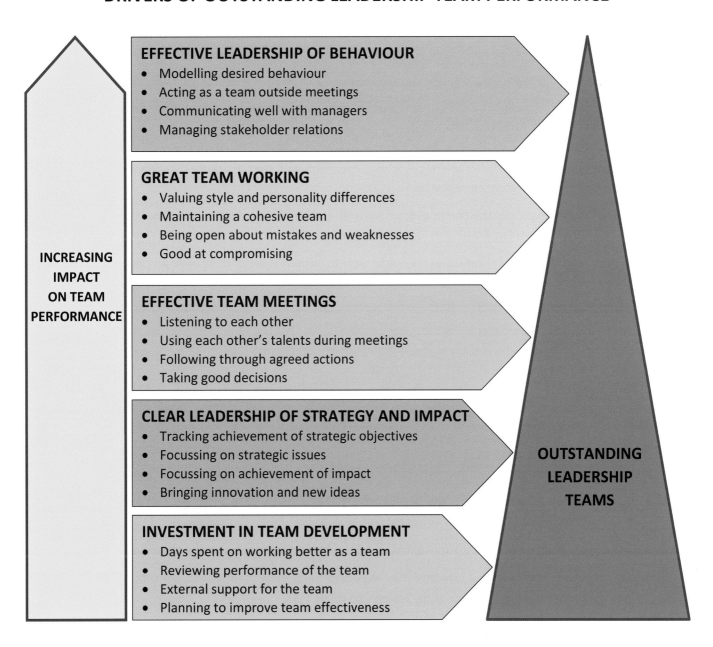

INCREASING IMPACT ON TEAM PERFORMANCE

EFFECTIVE LEADERSHIP OF BEHAVIOUR
- Modelling desired behaviour
- Acting as a team outside meetings
- Communicating well with managers
- Managing stakeholder relations

GREAT TEAM WORKING
- Valuing style and personality differences
- Maintaining a cohesive team
- Being open about mistakes and weaknesses
- Good at compromising

EFFECTIVE TEAM MEETINGS
- Listening to each other
- Using each other's talents during meetings
- Following through agreed actions
- Taking good decisions

CLEAR LEADERSHIP OF STRATEGY AND IMPACT
- Tracking achievement of strategic objectives
- Focussing on strategic issues
- Focussing on achievement of impact
- Bringing innovation and new ideas

INVESTMENT IN TEAM DEVELOPMENT
- Days spent on working better as a team
- Reviewing performance of the team
- External support for the team
- Planning to improve team effectiveness

OUTSTANDING LEADERSHIP TEAMS

Finally we investigated *which* charities had 'stronger' leadership teams. They were more likely to be:

- charities with higher income and more staff
- organisations where the chief executive had a greater breadth of experience
- more stable teams
- teams where are at least half are externally appointed members
- teams where more than two thirds are post graduates
- ethnically diverse teams.

Key conclusions

We drew the following conclusions from all of this research:

1. Leadership teams are critically important as they sit at the apex of organisations and have people with the skills and power to have a huge impact on the way organisations work and on their effectiveness.

2. The strongest drivers of the effectiveness of leadership teams are leadership of behaviour and great team working. They are followed by effective team meetings, leadership of strategy and impact and investment in team development.

3. Getting the right people of the team is a crucial starting point. Our research suggests chief executives should work towards smaller teams containing members with post graduate qualifications and then strive to maintain stable membership.

4. Team development was the component of leadership team working which was given the lowest performance rating, but it was also identified as one of the key future priorities.

5. Whilst two thirds of chief executives thought their teams were performing well, around a third felt their teams were only quite effective, so there is significant room for larger charities to improve the effectiveness of their leadership teams.

6. As far as we are aware this is the most comprehensive overview of leadership teams that has been created. Our approach provides an opportunity for organisations in the private and public sectors to learn from the experience of the charity sector.

Implications

We have identified implications for six key groups of people:

- For chief executives – the opportunity to benchmark their leadership team and pinpoint aspects requiring most attention

- For leadership team members – the opportunity to reflect on the strengths and weaknesses of their team and contribute to a culture of honest self-evaluation

- For board chairs – a framework for reflecting on the leadership team with the chief executive

- For board members – a reminder that their experience and judgement should contribute to thinking about the overall arrangements of the leadership team

- For HR directors – a framework for shaping leadership development programmes

- For senior managers – a prompt to provide their leadership team with formal and informal feedback on leadership team performance.

1　Introduction

Charities make a huge contribution to life in the UK. They provide a growing range of social welfare, health, housing, education, employment and international aid services and they champion important issues such as social justice, human rights, animal rights and the environmental protection. Every day organisations such as Citizens Advice, Macmillan Cancer Relief, Samaritans, Victim Support, Girlguiding, the Scouts, Shelter, WaterAid, WWF UK and thousands of smaller and less well known organisations are striving to improve the world we all live in.

The largest of these organisations now employ thousands of people, deliver services throughout the country, deploy huge volunteer workforces and raise and spend multi-million pound budgets every year. They are highly complex organisations often working in very challenging situations that place huge demands on their leadership and management.

These challenges are particularly acute for top management who have to juggle conflicting demands on their organisations whilst also dealing with sensitive ethical and public policy issues. The managers at the apex of the organisation, often called the leadership team, perform a crucial role in maximising the organisation's impact because they shape the most important decisions and have the power and authority to implement them.

Yet, surprisingly, remarkably little is known about these leadership teams:

- How are they structured?

- How stable is their membership?

- How well do they work as a team?

- What do they do to invest in their development?

- What do they do to provide leadership across their organisations?

More significantly there has been little research into what is most important in establishing outstandingly effective leadership teams.

We set out to answer these questions by investigating in detail the workings of the leadership teams of the UK's larger charities. It was immediately clear that leadership teams are complex entities and that their effectiveness depends on a wide range of structural and behavioural characteristics that need to be firmly in place for teams to operate at the highest levels.

We began by reviewing all the relevant literature and combined this with our experience and that of a valuable group of chief executives to pinpoint the 75 characteristics that might contribute to leadership team effectiveness. After combining some and disaggregating others we organised them into nine components of leadership team working. This is the research model that we used both to describe the key characteristics of leadership teams and to test the importance of each of them.

It is summarised below and set out in full in Appendix 6.

SUMMARY OF THE RESEARCH MODEL

LEADERSHIP TEAM

Organising the team	Managing the team	Leading the organisation
1. Team structure • Organisation design • Size of team • Roles on the team • Geographic location **2. Team membership** • Diversity • Internal/external appointment • Appointed by current CE • Tenure **3. Team leader** • Demographics • Previous experience • Tenure • Leadership of the team **4. Team recruitment and reward** • Selection • Flexibility of employment • Performance related pay	**5. Team meetings** • Types, frequency and duration • Agenda management • Behaviour in meetings • Decision quality • Following through actions **6. Team working** • Clarity of team purpose • Collective responsibility • Primacy of organisation interests • Cohesiveness • Openness and mutual trust • Ability to compromise **7. Team development** • Review of team performance • Plans to improve performance • Investing in team development • Team coaching and facilitation • CE team leadership skills • Departure from the team	**8. Leadership of strategy and impact** • Quantification of objectives • Wide understanding of objectives • Strategic focus • Responsiveness to change • Tracking performance • Managing risk • Focus on impact • Innovation and new ideas **9. Leadership of behaviour** • Expected behaviours • Establishing team values • Always acting as a team • Modelling desired behaviour • Cross organisation working • Learning culture • Working with the board • Chair CE relationship • Managing stakeholder relations • Communicating with managers

We used this structure to gather detailed information from 102 of the UK's top 500 charities about how teams are created and managed and how they lead their organisations. This allowed us to map the characteristics of leadership teams in detail.

We also wanted to understand how effective chief executives thought their organisations were at performing the nine components. So we invited them to rate how well their team performed on each component and to rate the overall effectiveness of their leadership team.

We then took this a step further and correlated the characteristics of leadership teams with overall effectiveness so we could identify which might be most important in building outstanding leadership teams. To make our analysis as robust as possible we looked at associations of characteristics to each of the components of leadership team performance and to the overall performance of the teams.

Of course we recognise that effective leadership teams are only one component of creating effective charities and that an effective leadership team might not equate to an effective charity. We did not attempt to identify relationships between effective teams and organisation health, finance or outcomes. However, our 30 years' experience of working with leadership teams, conversations with hundreds of managers and board members and the academic literature all point to the crucial importance of this group of people.

We viewed effectiveness of leadership teams as the *capacity* of its members to work together to maximise the *potential* of their charity to achieve its mission. Our assumption is that when charities have leadership teams with higher capacity to lead and manage their organisations, they are more likely to achieve their missions. Whilst this feels intuitively correct, we did not set out to prove this association.

We also recognise that different stakeholders may have entirely different views on the effectiveness of leadership teams and that leaders tend to regard their leadership more highly than their followers. We acknowledge that other team members, boards and staff might well have a very different perspective on the performance of their leadership team. In an ideal world we would have collected this information from a wider group of stakeholders but that would have been a much larger exercise than we could undertake. So to provide some limited corroboration we invited a sample of Human Resources (HR) directors in participating organisations to respond to the same rating questions that we asked of chief executives.

We further recognise the inherent limitations of self-assessment as those chief executives who have worked on developing leadership teams may believe that they have more effective teams just because they have done this work. However, HR director responses showed considerable consistency with chief executive views. Whilst HR directors generally gave a lower rating to leadership team performance, the pattern of responses was surprisingly similar to chief executive opinions.

We are also very aware that associations and correlations do not necessarily prove causality – they only indicate the existence of a relationship. We nevertheless take the view that knowing what other charities do and having an indication of actions that might contribute to strengthening leadership teams is better than having little or no evidence about what to do to increase their effectiveness.

Despite these potential limitations, we believe that by dividing leadership team arrangements into their component parts and quantifying how they work at present, we have created a framework for teams to benchmark themselves against other large charities so chief executives and team members can compare their team with a representative sample of the UK's larger charities.

The value of making such comparisons is that organisations can see whether their arrangements are typical or unusual, helping them to make judgements about their appropriateness. Furthermore, by identifying the characteristics that contribute most strongly to high performance, we have created a framework that can be used to pinpoint those improvements that will have the greatest leverage on team effectiveness.

Our earlier investigation of this type looked at charity governance, adopted a similar methodology and has been widely used to review the performance of charity governance. We hope that this latest research contributes to understanding how to make leadership teams more effective and therefore to the overall effectiveness of the charity sector.

The next three chapters of our report follow the structure of the research model: organising the team, managing the team and leading the organisation. Each chapter describes:

- The components of leadership teams we investigated

- How teams perform on these components

- What drives higher performance of these components

Chapter 5 then draws together all our findings and identifies the most important drivers of leadership team performance, how well they are performed and how prevalent they are across larger charities.

Chapter 6 draws conclusions and chapter 7 sets out some implications for leadership teams and their stakeholders.

We would welcome feedback which should be sent in the first instance to demerson@compassnet.co.uk

Summary of key terms

Term	Definition
Characteristics	The 75 dimensions that attempt to explain the performance of leadership teams in large UK charities.
Components	The nine groups of characteristics in the Compass Cass leadership team model: 1. Team membership 2. Team structure 3. Team leader 4. Team recruitment and reward 5. Team meetings 6. Team working 7. Team development 8. Leadership of strategy and performance 9. Leadership of behaviour across the organisation.
Drivers	The characteristics of leadership teams that our research found have the greatest impact in increasing the effectiveness of leadership teams.
Leadership team	The chief executive and the directors who meet regularly and take overall responsibility as a group for the strategic leadership of the organisation.

A full glossary can be found at Appendix 2.

2   Organising the team

The first pillar of the Compass Cass model of leadership teams is concerned with the overall organisation of the team. All organisations with a significant number of staff require some form of team at the top to provide leadership and management. Our preliminary research led us to think that four components with 20 characteristics might be significant in establishing an effective team, so we set out to explore each of these.

We will see later that although teams need to have a structure, members and a leader all of whom are adequately rewarded, none of the characteristics in this chapter such as organisation design, team size, diversity or reward turn out to be significant drivers of outstandingly effective teams.

We therefore see these components as the essential building blocks of effective teams rather than enablers of outstanding performance. In subsequent chapters we will report that the aspects which have greater impact in driving up overall performance are more concerned with behaviour and strategy than structures, people's background or their remuneration.

> **Summary of characteristics**
>
> **Team structure**
> - Organisation design
> - Size of team
> - Roles on the team
> - Geographic location
>
> **Team membership**
> - Diversity
> - Internal/external appointment
> - Appointed by current chief executive
> - Tenure
>
> **Team leader**
> - Demographics
> - Previous experience
> - Tenure
> - Leadership of the team
>
> **Team recruitment and reward**
> - Selection
> - Flexibility of employment
> - Performance related pay

2.1 Team structure

The structure of leadership teams varies widely across the sector. To ensure consistency of responses we defined the leadership team as the group in blue below:

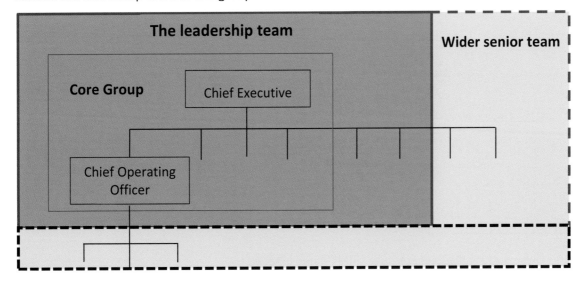

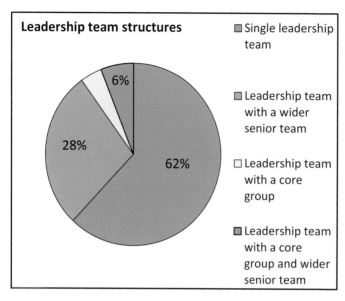

Leadership team structures

- Single leadership team
- Leadership team with a wider senior team
- Leadership team with a core group
- Leadership team with a core group and wider senior team

6%
28%
62%

Most organisations had a single leadership team. Only 4% had a 'core group' of directors within the leadership team, who might meet more regularly. However 28% had a leadership team with a 'wider senior team' of directors who report to the chief executive but are not part of the leadership team. A further 6% had both a core group and a wider senior team in their structure.

For those with a core group their average size was four members and for those with wider senior teams it was 15 people.[2]

Leadership teams varied widely in their size, structure, stability and geographic location.

Teams fell into three size bands:
- 19% Small leadership teams with 1 to 4 members
- 53% Medium-sized leadership teams with 5 to 7 members
- 26% Large leadership teams with 8 or more members.

Larger organisations had larger leadership teams. Organisations with more than 500 staff and organisations with income over £50m were more likely to have large teams.

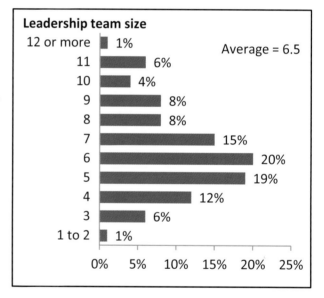

Leadership team size

Average = 6.5

Team size	Percentage
12 or more	1%
11	6%
10	4%
9	8%
8	8%
7	15%
6	20%
5	19%
4	12%
3	6%
1 to 2	1%

[2] Our figures always include the chief executive unless stated otherwise

The typical 'turnover' (or 'churn') in leadership team membership was one or two people every two years.

A third of teams had 3 or more new joiners in the last two years.

A minority (8%) of teams had a stable, unchanged membership over the last two years.

Number of new people joining the team in last 2 years	% of charities
None	8%
1-2	57%
3-4	26%
5 or more	8%
Not stated	1%

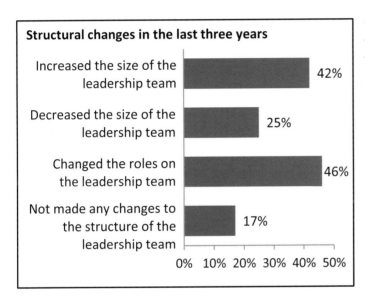

Structural changes in the last three years

Increased the size of the leadership team — 42%
Decreased the size of the leadership team — 25%
Changed the roles on the leadership team — 46%
Not made any changes to the structure of the leadership team — 17%

(0% 10% 20% 30% 40% 50%)

Over 80% had made any structural changes to their leadership team in the last three years. This was more often to change the team roles or to increase in size, rather than to decrease in size.

Chief executives with a long tenure of over 8 years were less likely to have made any changes in the last three years.

Chief executives leading small teams were the most likely to say they had decreased the size of their team recently and all of them thought their team size was now 'about right'.

In contrast half of large teams had increased in size in the last three years and only three quarters of their chief executives thought the current size was 'about right'; a quarter of them thought their team was too large. There was clearly a perception among team leaders that small teams were preferable.

Although the majority of chief executives had arrangements for deputising for their role, one in seven did not have any arrangements in place:

Arrangements for deputising for chief executive's role	% of charities
One member of the leadership team deputises for them	27%
The deputy role rotates around the team	21%
The leadership team includes a deputy chief executive	20%
Responsibilities are allocated across the team	16%
Other	3%
No arrangements in place	14%

The 20 organisations with a chief operating officer were asked which roles report to this post:

- 4 said directors responsible for internal functions (finance, HR, IT, property)
- 4 said directors responsible for service delivery
- 1 said all directors
- 7 said a mixture of the above
- 4 said 'other' arrangements.

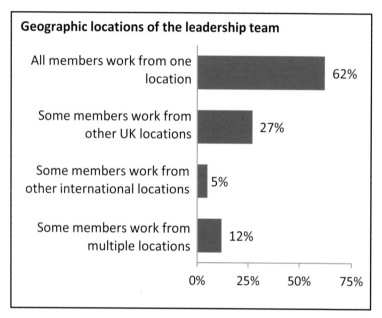

Geographic locations of the leadership team

Geographic location of team members can be a challenge for organisations operating across the UK and internationally. Members of teams were typically co-located but almost a third had some team members working from other UK or international locations.

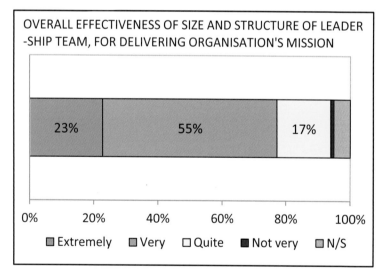

OVERALL EFFECTIVENESS OF SIZE AND STRUCTURE OF LEADER-SHIP TEAM, FOR DELIVERING ORGANISATION'S MISSION

Overall, 77% of chief executives thought the current size and structure of their leadership team was extremely or very effective for delivering the organisation's mission.

As team size increased, effectiveness of the size and structure of the leadership deal in delivering the organisation's mission reduced – further evidence that small teams were thought to be more effective.

Single most important action

When asked about the single most important action taken to strengthen the overall structure of their leadership team, some chief executives had added new roles, some had re-defined responsibilities of people on the team, some had reduced its size and some had dismissed weaker members. For the majority adjusting the membership of the team was their single most important action.

2.2 Team membership

Participants were asked to record the job titles and demographics for all their leadership team members, including themselves. Details were provided for 642 leadership team members.

There was a bewildering array of different job titles – over 100 distinct job titles were analysed. Job titles were therefore bundled together into 12 broader job function categories. The three most common job functions other than the chief executive were 'Director of Finance/ Corporate Services', 'Director of Fundraising/ Marketing/ Communications' and 'Director of a specific service or geographic territory'.

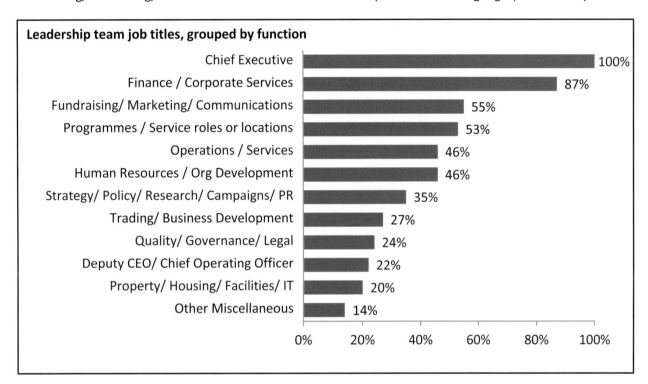

Leadership team job titles, grouped by function

Function	%
Chief Executive	100%
Finance / Corporate Services	87%
Fundraising/ Marketing/ Communications	55%
Programmes / Service roles or locations	53%
Operations / Services	46%
Human Resources / Org Development	46%
Strategy/ Policy/ Research/ Campaigns/ PR	35%
Trading/ Business Development	27%
Quality/ Governance/ Legal	24%
Deputy CEO/ Chief Operating Officer	22%
Property/ Housing/ Facilities/ IT	20%
Other Miscellaneous	14%

Tenure

The average tenure of leadership team members in an organisation was 5.2 years, so in a typical leadership team of 6.5 people this would result in a change of just over one person in the team each year.

Among the participating organisations 22% had leadership teams where all members were relatively recent joiners, having been in post no more than 5 years. In contrast, 31% of organisations had stable teams where all team members were long-standing, having been in post for 6 years or more. The remaining half had teams that comprised a mix of both newer and long-standing team members.

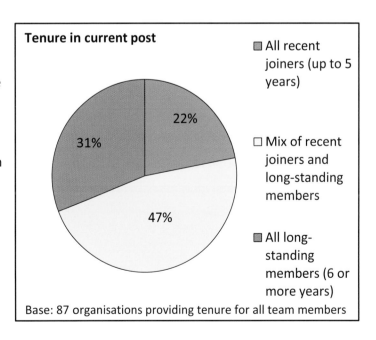

Tenure in current post

- 22% — All recent joiners (up to 5 years)
- 47% — Mix of recent joiners and long-standing members
- 31% — All long-standing members (6 or more years)

Base: 87 organisations providing tenure for all team members

Profile of leadership team members

We looked in detail at the team members to obtain an overview of their demographics. Team members were only slightly skewed towards men (55%). Ethnic minority representation (10%) was broadly comparable with the wider UK population. The vast majority of team members were degree educated and over a third had post graduate qualifications. Two-thirds were external appointments. Half of team members had been in post for no longer than 3 years and over two thirds were appointed by the current chief executive.

Demographics of leadership team members[3]		% of team members with each characteristic[4]
Gender	Male	55%
	Female	44%
Ethnic origin	White British	85%
	Other	10%
Highest educational attainment	Post graduate	36%
	Graduate	47%
	Non graduate	9%
Appointment	External appointment	66%
	Internal promotion	31%
Appointed by	Current chief executive	69%
	Chief executive's predecessors	21%
Working status	Full time	86%
	Part time	5%
Tenure – years in current post	1-3 years	48%
	4-7 years	24%
	8+ years	20%

We also looked at how transparent all of the top 500 charities were at publishing the details of their chief executives and leadership team members on their websites:

Chief executive's name was given by   83%

Chief executive's biographic details were given by 59%

Leadership team names were given by   66%

---

[3] Includes the chief executive except in the 'appointed by' row.

[4] There were 642 individual team members in total. A minority (2% - 10%) declined to answer on each demographic, so where percentages do not sum to 100% the residual were those who left the question blank.

In summary, a 'typical' leadership team might have:

- six members on the team, including a chief executive, a director of finance or corporate services, a director of fundraising/marketing/communications, a director of programmes or a specific service role or location, plus two other directors

- two or three women

- no one or one person from an ethnic minority

- two post graduates

- four individuals appointed externally

- three or four appointed by the current chief executive

- two 'long standing' members, having been in post for 6 years or more

- one member of the team working part time

- details of the team published on their website.

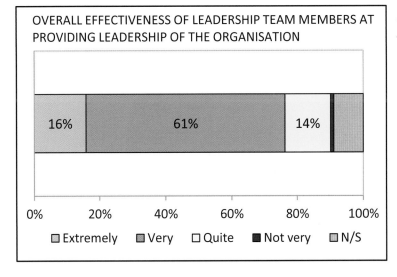

OVERALL EFFECTIVENESS OF LEADERSHIP TEAM MEMBERS AT PROVIDING LEADERSHIP OF THE ORGANISATION

Overall, 76% of chief executives thought the current membership of their leadership team was extremely or very effective at providing leadership of the organisation.

There were some variations in perceived effectiveness of leadership team members at providing leadership of the organisation by key demographics:

- Teams where fewer than half the team were external appointments were perceived to have a less effective membership than those in which more than half were external appointments.

- Teams with an above average proportion from ethnic minority reported higher than average team member effectiveness.

- The seven organisations with single gender teams were reported to have lower effectiveness.

2.3   The team leader

Two thirds (68%) of chief executives were men and one third (32%) were women.

83% were white British and 11% were from an ethnic minority (6% declined to answer).

The average age of chief executives was 54 years old. Men had a slightly younger age profile (54% aged less than 55 years) than women (45% aged less than 55 years old).

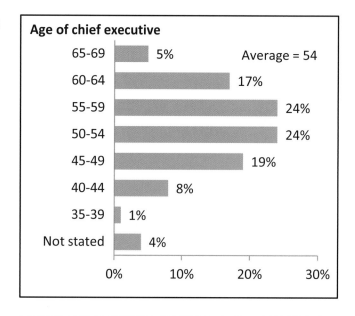

The majority (59%) of charity chief executives had a post graduate qualification. Estimates from research covering qualifications in the corporate sector suggest that this is similar or lower than the percentage of chief executives with postgraduate qualifications in FTSE 350 companies[5].

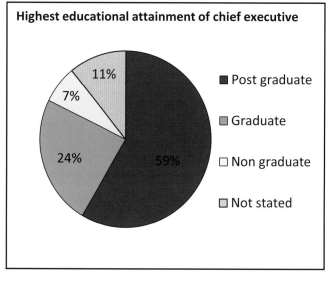

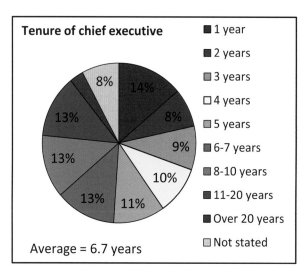

Chief executives had been in their current post for varying periods of time with an average tenure of 6.7 years. This is very similar to FTSE 350 companies where average tenure is 6.4 years.[5]

They fell into three groups by length of tenure:

- 'new' - in post for 1-3 years (30%)
- 'established' - 4-7 years tenure (33%)
- 'long-standing' - 8+ years (28%).

---

[5] FTSE 350 Board Review 2012, University of Southampton, 2012

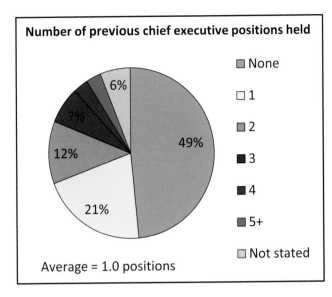

Number of previous chief executive positions held

- None
- 1
- 2
- 3
- 4
- 5+
- Not stated

49%
21%
12%
7%
6%

Average = 1.0 positions

Half of chief executives said they were in their first chief executive role, whilst 45% had held at least one previous chief executive position. There was an experienced quarter (25%) who had 2 or more previous chief executive positions behind them.[6]

Almost three quarters of chief executives were external appointments whereas a quarter was promoted internally to their current role. The proportions that were external appointments increased with increasing team size from 60% of chief executives leading small teams, to 89% of chief executives leading large teams.

For many years there has been speculation about the proportion of chief executives who have senior experience in the private and public sectors and those that are 'home grown' in the third sector. We analysed chief executives who recorded their past sector experience: 71% of them had previous experience of director or chief executive appointments within the third sector; 37% had had previous director or chief executive positions in the public sector and 31% in the private sector.

The small number of chief executives leading the largest charities with income over £100m were more likely than others to report previous experience at director level or above in the public sector (56%) or private sector (44%).

---

[6] There is a possibility that some may have come from senior civil service positions or divisional director level posts in large companies, and may not have identified this as previous 'chief executive experience' although they might have had a similar level of responsibility.

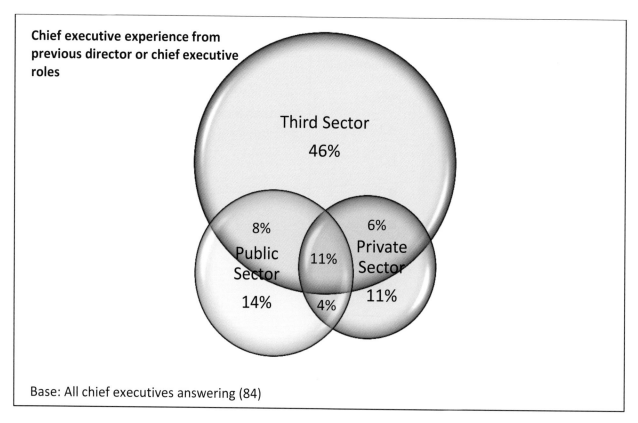

Chief executive experience from previous director or chief executive roles

Third Sector 46%

8% Public Sector 14%

11%

6% Private Sector 11%

4%

Base: All chief executives answering (84)

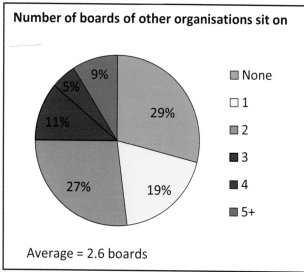

Number of boards of other organisations sit on

- None
- 1
- 2
- 3
- 4
- 5+

9%
5%
11%
27%
19%
29%

Average = 2.6 boards

71% of chief executives currently sat on the board of at least one other organisation.

Board members made input into chief executives' annual appraisal in 91% of organisations. Leadership team members did so in 43% of organisations.

Team leaders were asked what was the value of their remuneration, (including performance payments and employer's pension contribution) in the last 12 months. The modal salary was £100,000 - £125,000.

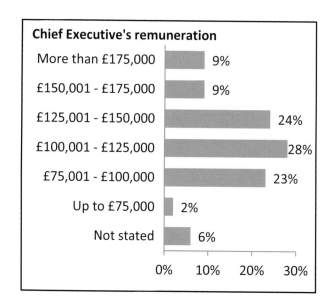

Chief Executive's remuneration

More than £175,000	9%
£150,001 - £175,000	9%
£125,001 - £150,000	24%
£100,001 - £125,000	28%
£75,001 - £100,000	23%
Up to £75,000	2%
Not stated	6%

0% 10% 20% 30%

We asked chief executives to assess how well they thought they performed various leadership functions related to the leadership team. They reported that they were most effective at delegating leadership responsibilities and admitting their mistakes to the rest of the team, and least effective at helping leadership team members to develop team working skills.

Rating of chief executive performance by HR directors was remarkably consistent with their own ratings, with the exception of delegating, where HR directors rated their chief executive's performance significantly lower.

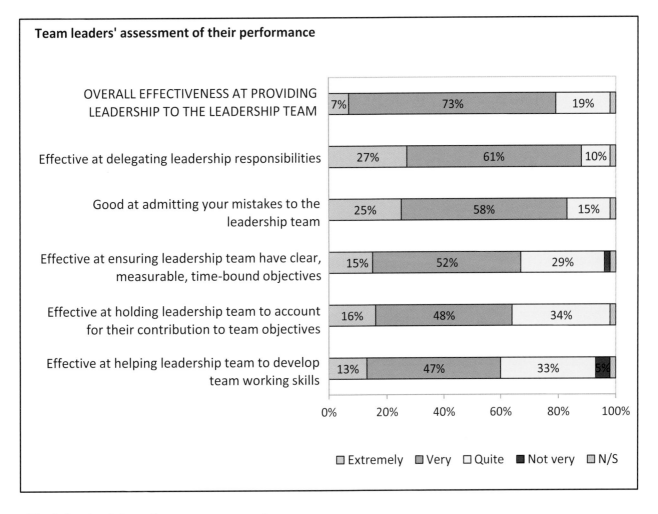

Team leaders' assessment of their performance

The following interactions were apparent:

- Chief executives with director level experience in the private or public sector thought they were better than those with only third sector experience at helping their colleagues to develop their team working skills and holding them to account for their contribution to team objectives.

- Female chief executives rated themselves more highly than their male counterparts on developing their team members' team working abilities and on admitting their own mistakes and weaknesses.

- Remuneration levels increased with organisation size, and so too did chief executives' perceived effectiveness on various leadership skills (listed in the chart above).

2.4 Recruitment and reward

Members of the leadership team were most often selected on the basis of a series of interviews and/or meetings with other existing members of the team. Half used personality tests and just under half used an assessment of 'fit' with other team members. Smaller teams used fewer different selection methods and were more likely to rely on just one interview rather than several.

Methods used to select people to join the leadership team	% of charities
Interviews on more than one occasion	83%
One or more meetings with other members of the leadership team	66%
Personality tests (such as SHL, Myers Briggs or 16PF)	50%
An assessment of 'fit' with other members of the team	47%
One or more meetings with the people they will manage	37%
An assessment centre	20%
Interviews on one occasion	18%
Other	6%

When appointing new leadership team members, the majority (82%) of charities offered some flexibility of working arrangements. Only a third offered part-time directorships but more than half offered the opportunity to work from home one day per week:

Flexible working arrangements offered when appointing team members	% of charities
Regularly working from home one day per week	58%
Opportunities to take additional time off work (unpaid)	44%
Working part-time	34%
Regularly working from home more than one day per week	22%
Other	9%
Don't offer flexible working arrangements	15%

Performance related pay is a controversial topic in charities. Our research showed that over 40% of larger charities have any form of performance-related payments for leadership team members:

Performance-related payments made to any members of the leadership team	% of charities
All members of the team are eligible for performance-related payments	31%
Some members of the team receive a performance-related payment	9%
No member of the team receives a performance-related payment	54%
The payment is related to personal performance	18%
The payment is related to organisation performance	16%
The payment is related to contribution to the leadership team	6%
Other	4%

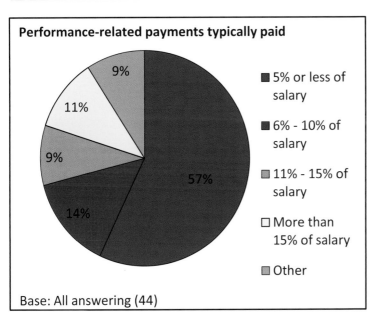

Performance-related payments typically paid

- 5% or less of salary
- 6% - 10% of salary
- 11% - 15% of salary
- More than 15% of salary
- Other

Base: All answering (44)

When asked about the scale of performance-related payments typically paid to leadership team members, most said the performance-related payments were typically 5% or less of salary. A third of those answering said the payments were more than 5%.

Larger teams were more likely to use performance related pay and when they did it was more likely to be linked to individuals' contribution to leadership team performance.

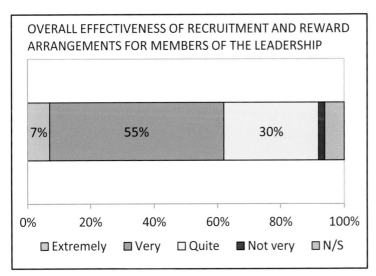

OVERALL EFFECTIVENESS OF RECRUITMENT AND REWARD ARRANGEMENTS FOR MEMBERS OF THE LEADERSHIP

7% 55% 30%

0%   20%   40%   60%   80%   100%

☐ Extremely ☐ Very ☐ Quite ☐ Not very ☐ N/S

Overall 62% of chief executives thought that the recruitment and reward arrangements they had in place for members of the leadership team were extremely or very effective.

Chief executives of larger organisations (with income over £50m) reported that they had more effective recruitment and reward arrangements.

Single most important actions in recruitment and reward

When asked about the single most important action they had taken to strengthen recruitment and reward chief executives said, in order of most mentions:

- benchmarking pay against comparable organisations

- introducing flexible working arrangements

- introducing performance related pay

- appointing a director of human relations.

Drivers for organising effective leadership teams

When we looked at the relationships between reported effectiveness in each of the four components of organising leadership teams we found that the characteristics that were most closely associated with higher performing teams were:

- a smaller team, with a simple leadership team structure and co-located

- a stable team, with low turnover in membership

- with a high proportion of post graduates

- with at least half the members being externally appointed

- offering performance related payments to team members

- the team leader's tenure and breadth of experience.

Commentary

Getting the right people on the team is clearly an essential starting point for any chief executive wanting to create an effective leadership team. However, decisions to change the membership of the leadership team clearly have to be balanced against other considerations including maintaining team stability and retaining members who hold the organisation's history, introducing people with new and different perspectives and ensuring the team does not become stale.

People who are appointed as members of leadership teams need to recognise that this is a significant promotion. As well as having to have the necessary functional expertise to direct the division of an organisation, members have to:

- understand the broader context in which the organisation works

- have a strategic overview of the organisation as a whole

- understand how to work with the board and

- be able to contribute to the smooth working of the leadership team.

These all take time to achieve and point to the importance of chief executives ensuring that new team members all receive a well-planned induction.

Whilst new members are striving to do all of this, the rest of the team has to adjust to the arrival of a new member, understand their strengths and weaknesses and learn to accommodate their style and personality. This requires time and effort from the rest of the leadership team.

Our research suggests that once chief executives have a competent team in place, they should strive for reasonable stability and pay close attention to the development needs and personal aspirations of team members. Whilst organisations have to accept that good people will seek promotion and new challenges, the disruption caused by changes to the leadership team is significant. The fact that a quarter of leadership teams in our research had 3-4 changes in the last two years, suggest that there is potential to reduce churn in leadership team membership across large charities as a whole.

We also note that team leaders report small teams to be more effective. However, 42% of organisations reported that they had increased team size in the last three years. There is clearly a temptation to solve problems by adding new positions on the team, even though there may be a price to pay in terms of team effectiveness.

We were surprised to find that although third sector leadership teams have a considerably better gender balance than those in the private and public sectors, gender was not associated with reported performance of the team, except in single gender teams. This contradicts the finding from the wider literature and from our previous research into governance which pointed to diversity as a driver of performance.

Finally, we note that although there has been considerable enthusiasm for appointing chief operating officers in recent years, amongst those teams that had this role there was no association with *very* good team performance but there was an association with *extremely* good performance, suggesting that where this role worked extremely well it made a significant difference to team performance.

3 Managing the team

The second pillar of the Compass Cass model of leadership teams is about the way teams work and develop their capacity to be more effective. There are three components here and our preliminary research suggested that there might be 34 possible characteristics.

Team meetings are an essential part of team life, so we began by mapping out how they are organised and reviewed. We then looked at how teams work together and finally at what they do to develop team effectiveness.

As we will see later, these components of managing leadership teams contribute significantly to building successful teams and some of their characteristics will be shown to be amongst the most important drivers of outstanding leadership teams.

Summary of characteristics

Team meetings
- Types, frequency and duration
- Agenda management
- Behaviour in meetings
- Decision quality
- Following through actions

Team working
- Clarity of team purpose
- Collective responsibility
- Primacy of organisation interests
- Cohesiveness
- Openness and mutual trust
- Ability to compromise

Team development
- Review of team performance
- Plans to improve team performance
- Investing in team development
- Team coaching and facilitation
- CE team leadership skills
- Departure from the team

3.1 Team meetings

Meetings are an important part of the lives of leadership team members and few are more important than those of the leadership team itself. We therefore wanted to explore the types and frequencies of meetings, how members behave in meetings and which characteristics contributed most to meeting effectiveness.

On average, leadership teams spent 15 days in all types of leadership team meetings per year.

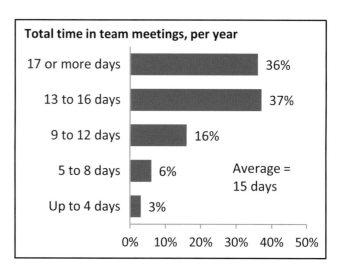

Total time in team meetings, per year

17 or more days	36%
13 to 16 days	37%
9 to 12 days	16%
5 to 8 days	6%
Up to 4 days	3%

Average = 15 days

The majority of organisations held a variety of different types of meetings.

Usually leadership team meetings were chaired by the chief executive (89%). 5% said that another specified team member acted as the chair and 4% said the chair role rotated among the team members.

Types of meetings	% of charities
Brief catch up and co-ordination	75%
Operational management	82%
Strategic management	84%
Strategy 'away day'	92%

'Away day' type meetings where teams focus for an extended period on topics such as longer term strategy, team development and organisation behaviour are part of the life of many leadership teams. Three quarters of teams spent 1-4 days in 'away days' annually, whilst 16% spent 5 or more.

Days spent in 'away day' meetings in a typical year	% of charities
None	8%
1 - 2 days	45%
3 – 4 days	31%
5 – 6 days	9%
7 or more days	7%

Two thirds of leadership teams met face-to-face at least fortnightly. Although much talked about, virtual meetings were still used relatively rarely and over half never did so.

Frequency of meetings	Face-to-face	Tele-conference/ video
Weekly	39%	14%
Fortnightly	26%	5%
Monthly	28%	4%
Every other month	3%	2%
Less frequently	2%	19%
Never	n/a	56%

Reviewing meeting effectiveness

Six in seven leadership teams reviewed team meeting performance in a variety of ways. Performance during meetings was more often evaluated during individuals' appraisals than collectively in a formal annual review, or informally at the end of meetings. However, the more different methods of evaluation were adopted, the higher was the perceived overall effectiveness of team meetings; this suggests that teams which invest more time and effort into reviewing their performance during meetings ultimately achieved more productive meetings.

Methods of reviewing performance in leadership team meetings	% of charities
Team contribution is part of individual appraisals	58%
Formally review the performance of team meetings at least once a year	36%
Quick review at the end of each meeting	19%
Other	5%

Overall, 68% of chief executives thought that the meetings of their leadership team were extremely or very effective. Perceived effectiveness of team meetings was higher in organisations with higher income, if the chief executive had a greater breadth of experience and in more established teams (when all members had more than three years in post).

Chief executives were asked to rate performance on seven different dimensions of team meetings. Quality of decision making was a perceived strength: 82% rated this aspect extremely/very good. The two weakest dimensions were ensuring that agendas were tightly controlled and making best use of each other's talents during meetings – fewer than half of organisations rated these extremely or very highly.

Leadership Team meetings

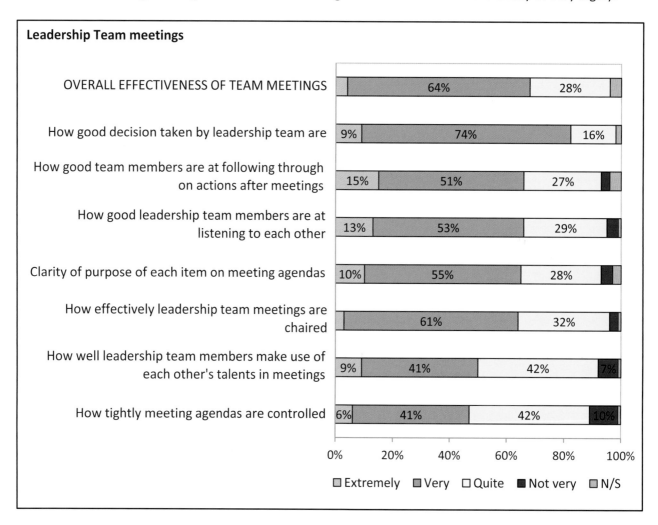

Drivers of effective team meetings

The following were most strongly associated with high ratings of overall effectiveness of leadership team meetings:

- listening to each other well during meetings

- making good use of each other's talents during meetings

- following through on actions taken after meetings

- taking good decisions.

Single most important actions

When asked about the single most important action they had taken to develop their teams, chief executives overwhelmingly reported actions to strengthen planning of meeting agendas and the quality and timeliness of papers. Other actions were (in order of most frequently mentioned) included:

- work on behaviour in meetings including openness and 'living' organisation values

- being systematic about taking and tracking actions

- separating out different types of meetings.

Commentary

The drivers of effective meetings are all important behaviours that chief executives can encourage. Chief executives generally chair meetings so can ensure that everyone is heard and that everyone's' contributions are valued. Team members can assist by sharing responsibility for asking for other members' views and valuing their responses.

Having great meetings can be stimulating and rewarding. Following through on agreed actions can be tougher and more tedious, but the association we found with better meetings and the frequent mention of 'follow through' as the single most important action chief executives had taken suggests that this requires dedicated attention.

Although it may sometimes be delegated as an administrative task, the agenda can be a significant determinant of how meeting time is spent. Our findings suggest that it is a matter that deserves close attention. Both the chief executive and the team as a whole should regularly review the forward agenda plan.

CASE STUDY- Different types of meetings at Fremantle

Fremantle, a charity that provides high quality care services for older and disabled people recently re-structured its leadership teams meetings. Every other month the team holds an information exchange meeting, finishing with a round up that identifies burning issues. These issues are not discussed but the team agrees who will prepare papers on the issue for the subsequent meeting. Briefing papers are circulated in advance so that at the alternate meeting the team discusses and resolves issues rather than spending time getting informed about the problem. The Chief Executive reports that having different types of meetings is working well and has improved focus on delivering key outcomes and contributed to better teamwork.

3.2   Team working

Working as a team is a complex and delicate matter. Leadership teams need to be able to have robust discussions in private and at the same time work together in a wide range of public settings. Members of the team have to provide leadership of their own departments and at the same time put corporate priorities above divisional interests. Many team activities have the potential to create tension and conflict. Although team meetings and team working overlap, we wanted to get some insights into how teams worked outside the setting of formal meetings.

The majority had discussed the team's purpose and how they want to work together. Half had clarified their expectations of each other but only a third had discussed response to unacceptable behaviour.

Actions taken by leadership team in last 3 years to define its purpose and expected behaviours	% of charities
Discussed how we want to work together	75%
Discussed why we do what we do as a team	66%
Discussed why the leadership team exists	60%
Discussed what we expect of each other	52%
Discussed how we respond to transgressions to agreed behaviours	34%
Other	4%

Two thirds of chief executives would like the leadership team to spend the same amount of time working together in future, as they did last year; a quarter would like to more time working as a team, and only 4% would prefer less time.

In terms of how time spent working as a team is allocated, chief executives typically would like to spend more time in future on managing strategic performance and developing the team and around the same amount of time on other activities. Around a quarter indicated that they would like to spend less time on directing operations or on governance.

Desired allocation of time on different activities, in future

Participants were asked to rate performance on 11 different dimensions of team working. There were five characteristics where performance was particularly strong: clarity of purpose, openness and mutual trust, passionate strategic debate, putting organisation impact above departmental interests and collective responsibility for decisions. The weakest aspects of team working were valuing each other's style and personality differences and willingness to call each other to account for counter-productive behaviours.

Team Working

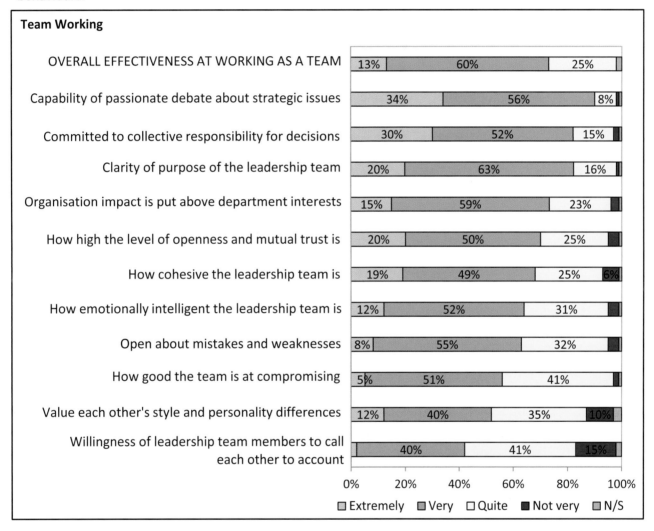

The following interactions were apparent:

- Chief executives with a greater breadth of experience rated their teams more highly on the leadership team's clarity of purpose, cohesiveness, collective responsibility for decisions, emotional intelligence and willingness to call each other to account for counter-productive behaviours.

- The better the chief executive was at admitting their own mistakes and weaknesses, the more open the leadership team was about mistakes and weaknesses.

Drivers of effective team working

All the team working characteristics we explored were associated with higher team working performance. There were consistently strong links between doing well on each and doing well at team working overall; participants clearly recognised the value of getting all facets of team working right.

The following four drivers were *most* strongly associated with high ratings on overall effectiveness of leadership team members working as a team:

- good at genuinely valuing each other's style and personality differences

- high team cohesiveness

- openness about mistakes and weaknesses

- good at compromising.

Single most important actions

The most frequently mentioned action taken to improve team working was to allocate time to team development usually working with an external coach or facilitator, sometimes as part of a leadership development programme. A few chief executives reported that the single most important action they had taken to improve team working was to change the membership of the team.

Commentary

More than a third of participants gave their teams a low performance rating on three characteristics that were drivers of outstanding teams: genuinely valuing style and personality differences, being open about mistakes and compromising. Our consultancy experience tells us that whilst it is challenging for teams to excel in these behaviours, spending time openly discussing the purpose of the team, how to value each other and be open about mistakes leads to more effective team working.

Willingness to call each other to account was the weakest aspect of team working (over half gave a low rating of only quite or not very good); this is a feature of high functioning teams that is not easy to achieve. It requires a high level of trust and openness to discussing when and how it should be done. Good foundations for these discussions can be established by discussing how the team wants to work together and what behaviours the team wishes to exhibit when working together.

3.3   Team development

All teams need to invest in themselves, so we asked a number of questions about team development. As will become apparent in this section, leaders take many actions to develop their teams. However, both chief executives and HR directors rated performance on team development the lowest of all the components of an effective leadership team. They clearly did not think that their organisations were good at team development.

Individual development

In terms of investing in the development of individuals on the team, over 60% of leadership teams had used any psychological test in the last three years to gain insights into individuals and the roles they play.

Psychological tests used in the last three years	% of charities
Myers Briggs Type indicators	45%
Belbin's Team Roles	22%
Another test	15%
No tests used in last 3 years	36%

Chief executives typically had one-to-one meetings with their leadership team members monthly:

Regularity of individual, face-to-face meetings	% of charities
Weekly	20%
Monthly	71%
Every other month	3%
Quarterly	4%

Five in six chief executives had taken action within the last three years to support any under-performing members of their leadership team, most often by having very direct conversations with them about the need for improvement. Practical support offered was most likely to be coaching, followed by support from a trustee, followed by shadowing a peer.

Actions taken by chief executive to support under-performing members of the leadership team in the last three years	% of charities
Had very direct conversations with them about improving performance	74%
Asked them to have a coach	52%
Given them a written warning about improving performance	35%
Asked a board member to give them one-to-one support	28%
Suggested they shadow a director in another organisation	15%
None of the above	10%

84% of chief executives had taken any actions.

Three quarters of chief executives had taken any of the actions listed below to get someone to leave the leadership team; this was most often agreed mutually or by a compromise / settlement agreement:

Actions taken by chief executive in the last three years to get a member to leave the leadership team	% of charities
Mutually agreed departure	58%
Compromise agreement	48%
Restructuring of roles or responsibilities	45%
Early retirement	23%
Other	4%
No such actions in last three years	22%

Team development actions

Over 80% of charities had taken at least one action to invest in leadership team development recently. Three quarters had utilised external assistance to support team development and a fifth had conducted a (formal) review of team performance[7]; fewer had reviewed their performance using internal resource:

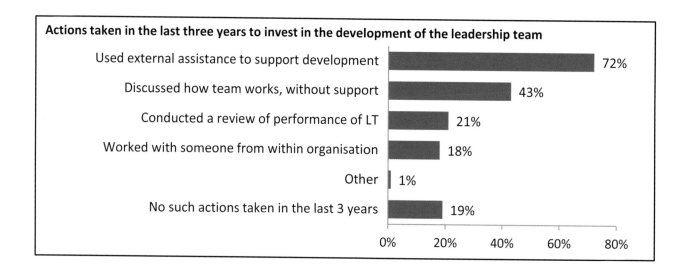

Actions taken in the last three years to invest in the development of the leadership team

- Used external assistance to support development: 72%
- Discussed how team works, without support: 43%
- Conducted a review of performance of LT: 21%
- Worked with someone from within organisation: 18%
- Other: 1%
- No such actions taken in the last 3 years: 19%

---

[7] There were more people who went on to say what their formal review entailed without confirming whether this was in the last 3 years; including these as well takes the tally to 56% who had ever conducted a formal review of leadership team performance. Given the average chief executive tenure was 6.7 years, most of these reviews would probably have been within that timeframe.

Time spent in last 12 months working better as a team	% of charities
None	18%
Up to half a day	13%
More than half, up to 1 day	26%
More than 1, up to 2 days	21%
More than 2 days	22%

In terms of investing in the development of the team collectively only a third of leadership teams invested more than one day per year in developing their team working skills.

Chief executives who had been in post for longer reported that their team spent less time on team development.

Only a fifth reported that they had conducted a review of team performance in the last 3 years and only half (56%) had ever undertaken such a review.

Reviews were most likely to include one-to-one meetings between the reviewer and individual team members, then input from people reporting to team members, then input from board members or wider staff and least likely to incorporate input from external stakeholders:

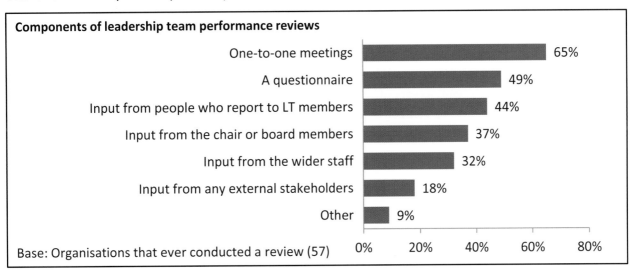

Components of leadership team performance reviews

- One-to-one meetings — 65%
- A questionnaire — 49%
- Input from people who report to LT members — 44%
- Input from the chair or board members — 37%
- Input from the wider staff — 32%
- Input from any external stakeholders — 18%
- Other — 9%

Base: Organisations that ever conducted a review (57)

Leadership teams that had used external support for team development most often used an external facilitator in training sessions; fewer used a team coach:

Components of external support for leadership development (in last three years)

- Held externally facilitated training sessions — 79%
- Team coach acted as process consultant in meetings — 37%
- Team coach supported team development over 6 or more months — 30%
- Other — 5%

Base: Organisations that had external support (73)

To help improve their own team leadership skills, chief executives had most often discussed this with their chair. A third had taken a coach and a third a mentor.

Actions taken by chief executives to develop their own 'team leadership skills' in the last three years	% of charities
Discussed their team leadership skills with their chair	59%
Have a coach	33%
Have a mentor	32%
Done training specifically on their team leadership skills	27%
Member of an action learning set	13%
Other	4%
No actions taken	13%

87% of chief executives had taken any actions.

Overall, the performance in team development was by far the lowest rated of the various components investigated. No chief executives rated their team as extremely effective at team development and only a third (32%) rated their team as very effective. Over half (60%) of chief executives acknowledged that they were only quite or not very effective. Chief executives clearly think that their performance on team development lags behind their performance on all the other components in our model.

The third who rated coaches they had used were complimentary: 76% thought it was extremely or very valuable to team development. But performance ratings were particularly low on plans for improving team effectiveness and celebrating success; these were the two lowest scoring dimensions across the survey.

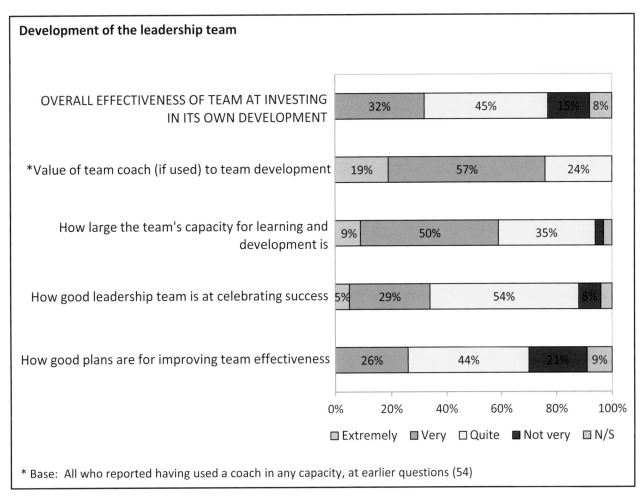

Development of the leadership team

OVERALL EFFECTIVENESS OF TEAM AT INVESTING IN ITS OWN DEVELOPMENT: 32% | 45% | 15% | 8%

*Value of team coach (if used) to team development: 19% | 57% | 24%

How large the team's capacity for learning and development is: 9% | 50% | 35%

How good leadership team is at celebrating success: 5% | 29% | 54% | 8%

How good plans are for improving team effectiveness: 26% | 44% | 21% | 9%

Legend: □ Extremely ■ Very □ Quite ■ Not very □ N/S

* Base: All who reported having used a coach in any capacity, at earlier questions (54)

Drivers of team development

The following were most strongly associated with high ratings of overall effectiveness of the leadership team investing in its own development:

- more than one day spent in the last 12 months specifically on working better as a team

- leadership team performance review, including input from three or more different sources

- using external support for team development, including a team coach

- good plans for improving the effectiveness of the team.

Single most important actions

Chief executives said the single most important action they had taken to develop their teams were (in order of most frequently mentioned):

- appointing a coach for individuals or the team as a whole

- instigating a leadership development programme

- working on behaviours, values and openness

- taking time out for team development.

Commentary

Making significant investment in leadership team development is a comparatively new activity for charity leadership teams. Some teams may feel reluctant to spend hard won charitable funds on themselves or to allocate time to it when they are facing many other pressures. Our research shows that some organisations have put time and effort into it, but most are not particularly satisfied with the effectiveness of this investment.

Performance in team development was given the lowest rating of all the components in our model leaving us wondering whether that might be because it is hard to do it really well, whether insufficient time or resources were allocated to it, or it did not have the desired impact. For some organisations we suspect that it may be important that team development is delivered in ways that reflect the culture and complexity of their organisations, particularly those with a strong voluntary ethos.

Despite this, many chief executives reported that investing time and having external support for team development was their single most important action in this area. Actions such as having a team coach were reported by many to be valuable and the number of different actions that had been taken to invest in team development did correlate with team development. This leads us to think that it is an important component of team effectiveness, but that it needs significant investment of time and effort to do it well.

CASE STUDY- Team development at Samaritans

When the Chief Executive of Samaritans joined the organisation, the leadership team consisted of seven directors and twelve heads of departments that met monthly. The directors also met separately twice a month and the heads of department met less regularly. A review by an independent consultant led to a re-structuring of meetings including replacement of the heads of department meetings with monthly meetings of directors with their teams.

In parallel Samaritans embarked on leadership development for all senior managers. After a false start with a leadership training provider, they decided to create their own bespoke programme using inputs from carefully selected experts on some topics and skills based training on others. Catherine Johnstone, the Chief Executive, also procured six individual coaching sessions pro bono for all seven directors and expected all of them to be used.

She reported that the leadership team:

- valued being invested in, particularly during economically tough times for the organisation

- is now a much more coherent and intuitive team willing to provide stronger leadership whilst seeking approval less frequently

- is taking greater responsibility, freeing her up to be more externally facing.

---

4   Leading the organisation

The third pillar of the Compass Cass model is about teams' responsibilities for leading their organisations. This section investigates two components of effectiveness and their 21 characteristics.

When we were exploring potential characteristics of leadership teams at the outset of this research, chief executives told us that providing leadership on strategy and on behaviour across the organisation were two of the team's most important functions. We therefore included both of these components in our model and asked questions about what teams did and how well they did them.

As we shall see later, leadership of behaviour across the organisation turned out to be the strongest driver of outstanding leadership teams.

4.1   *Leadership of strategy and impact*

All of the participants said they had organisation-wide strategic objectives in place and three quarters said all or most of these were quantified and time-bound. However a residual fifth reported that only a few or none of their objectives were quantified and time-bound:

How quantified and time-bound are organisation-wide strategic objectives	% of charities
None are quantified and time-bound	5%
A few are quantified and time-bound	16%
Most are quantified and time-bound	49%
All are quantified and time-bound	27%

Summary of characteristics

Leadership of strategy and impact
- Quantification of objectives
- Wide understanding of objectives
- Strategic focus
- Responsiveness to change
- Tracking performance
- Managing risk
- Focus on impact
- Innovation and new ideas

Leadership of behaviour
- Expected behaviours
- Establishing team values
- Always acting as a team
- Modelling desired behaviour
- Cross organisation working
- Learning culture
- Working with the board
- Chair CE relationship
- Managing stakeholder relations
- Communicating with managers

Leadership teams typically reviewed both strategic performance and the risk register on a quarterly basis:

Frequency of reviewing:	Performance systemically against strategic objectives	Risk register
Monthly	12%	24%
Quarterly	49%	51%
Half yearly	19%	11%
Annually	16%	14%

Overall, 74% of chief executives considered their team to be extremely or very effective at delivering leadership of the organisation's strategy and performance; and as their tenure lengthened, so did their rating on this aspect of leadership.

Chief executives rated how well the team leads the organisation's strategy and impact on 10 different characteristics. The ratings were very high on team members being in complete agreement about the organisation's strategic objectives and on tracking financial performance (these were among the highest performance ratings given across all dimensions in the survey). In contrast, the weakest aspects were ensuring strategic objectives were understood across the organisation, effectively tracking achievement of strategic objectives and bringing new ideas to the organisation.

Drivers of leading strategy and impact

The following characteristics of leadership teams were most strongly associated with high ratings on overall effectiveness at delivering leadership of the organisation's strategy and impact:

- being highly effective at tracking the achievement of strategic objectives

- having a sharp focus on strategic issues

- being highly focussed on achievement of impact

- being good at innovation and bringing new ideas into the organisation.

Single most important actions

The single most important actions taken by chief executives to strengthen strategy and impact were (in order of most mentions):

- creating clearer and briefer missions and plans

- establishing and streamlining systems to improve reporting on performance against objectives

- using balanced scorecards

- communicating goals and achievements.

Commentary

Strategy development has been on charity leadership team agendas for many years. Our research shows that the challenge of creating and communicating really clear strategies continues to be a priority for leadership teams. These days there is greater emphasis on creating quantified and time bound strategic objectives and on regular review of achievements. The fact that three quarters report that all or most of their strategic objectives were quantified and time bound reflects a dramatic improvement over recent years.

Many organisations are now striving to track strategic achievements more effectively. Our experience suggests that this is particularly difficult in organisations that are geographically dispersed and those that both deliver services and campaign for changes in public policy. We are aware that some organisations have become much better at capturing good information about their outputs and outcomes in a regular and systematic way and reporting it on summary 'scorecards' containing a range of different types of indicators.

Nevertheless this research still finds that chief executives reporting that their organisations are better at tracking financial performance and managing risk than they are on tracking strategic achievements. Further investment in this area is likely to reap significant rewards as it was the characteristic that correlated most closely with effectiveness in delivering strategy and impact.

4.2   Leadership of behaviour across the organisation

Behaviours, beliefs and values underpin much of what people do in organisations. Managers, staff and volunteers watch the behaviour of their leaders to see what is important to them, how they use their time and how they respond to different circumstances. So we wanted to look at what teams did to provide leadership of behaviour across their organisations.

The vast majority of leadership teams had taken some steps to establish values and behaviours more widely across the organisation and strive to ensure their actions are consistent with organisation values. However, only 30% said that breaches of organisation values by leadership team members were swiftly dealt with.

Actions taken by leadership team in last three years to establish values and behaviours more widely across the organisation	% of charities
Our values are widely promoted and regularly referred to	74%
Strive to ensure our actions are always consistent with our values	73%
Periodically discuss the organisation's values and behaviours	71%
Breaches of organisation values are dealt with swiftly and diligently	30%
Other	2%
Not taken any specific actions to promote values and behaviours	4%

95% of charities had taken any actions and 25% had taken four or more actions.

In all large organisations there is a natural tendency for departments to begin to give greater attention to departmental work and priorities, sometimes to the detriment of the organisation as a whole. Our research showed that 85% of chief executives encouraged cross organisation teams and almost three quarters took the bolder step of having periodic meetings of most top managers in their organisations – actions that are likely to encourage integration and more consistent behaviour across their organisations.

Actions taken in last three years to encourage cross-organisation working	% of charities
Actively encourage cross organisation teams	85%
Periodically have a meeting of most top managers in the organisation	72%
Actively discourage any 'silo mentality'	65%
Not taken any such actions	1%

Overall, 68% of chief executives considered their team to be extremely or very effective at delivering leadership of behaviour across the organisation; and chief executives with a greater breadth of experience and a longer tenure reported better performance on this aspect of leadership.

Chief executives rated seven different aspects of leadership of behaviour. Relationships between management and governance were a relative strength: most chief executives were very positive about their relationship with the chair of the board (one of the highest performance ratings given across all dimensions in the survey), and they also rated relationships between leadership team members and board members positively. The lowest rating was given to systematic management of relationships with all stakeholders.

Leadership of behaviour across the organisation

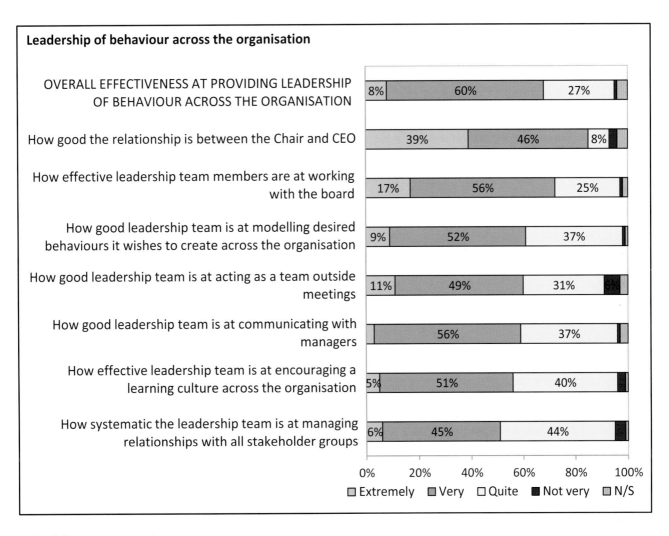

The following interactions were apparent:

- Smaller teams scored more highly than medium-sized or large teams on all dimensions charted above; apart from managing stakeholder relations, where medium-sized and larger teams performed better.

- Chief executives with a greater breadth of experience gave an above average rating to relating to the chair and the rest of the board, and with other managers outside the leadership team.

Drivers of leading behaviour across the organisation

The following characteristics of leadership teams were most strongly associated with high ratings on overall effectiveness at providing leadership of behaviour across the organisation:

- good at modelling the desired behaviours the team wish to create across the organisation

- good at acting as a team outside team meetings

- good at communicating with managers across the whole organisation

- highly systematic at managing relationships with all stakeholder groups.

Single most important actions

The single most important actions taken by chief executives to strengthen leadership team behaviour were (in order of most mentions):

- taking time to clarify values and expected behaviours

- improving communications across the organisation

- establishing training and leadership development programmes.

Commentary

The behaviour of leadership teams is watched more closely than team members sometimes realise. To be credible in providing leadership of behaviour across their organisations, leadership teams need to have clarified and understood the behaviours they expect of each other and how they will live up to their standards. This is one of the most challenging aspects of being a member of a leadership team.

The highest levels of trust are needed to open up discussion about the values the team wishes to espouse and the personal behaviours that are expected of team members. This requires a stable team membership that has the basic elements of team working in place, that has delegated many operational matters to a competent team of managers and so has the time to devote attention to this area.

Leadership of behaviour is particularly challenging in organisations with a large volunteer workforce and those that have a strong ethos, sometimes related directly to the nature of their mission. The managerial assumptions that people at the top of the organisation make sometimes sit uncomfortably alongside the values of people delivering front line services. So the best leadership teams make time 'walk the talk', get out to the front line and connect in as many ways as possible with stakeholders, particularly in organisations with nations, regions or branches.

This can be supplemented by staff and volunteer surveys to gauge opinion across the organisation and 360° performance reviews of the leadership team, so the team gets accurate information about how their 'followers' rate their performance.

Our research suggests that working on leadership of behaviour across the organisation can have a significant impact on leadership team effectiveness. It helps to mobilise the whole organisation to work in similar ways to achieve the mission that all stakeholders share.

CASE STUDY- Learning and development at Leukaemia & Lymphoma Research

Progress in blood cancer research meant that Leukaemia & Lymphoma Research (LLR) faced an unprecedented opportunity to achieve greater impact. LLR believed that a greater contribution was needed from everyone and that this could be achieved through a learning and development programme. The justification for this investment was the desired increase in the organisation's impact.

The initial focus was on the development of Directors and Heads of Departments, starting by exploring personal beliefs and values. The programme used Myers Briggs Type Indicators to help managers make choices and decisions about behaviour. The resulting culture of feedback enabled managers to explore how to make the most of their strengths and consequently drive good performance

The Leadership Team is now using Patrick Lencioni's 'Five Dysfunctions of a Team' to increase trust in each other, engage in unfiltered conflict around ideas and hold each other more accountable.

As an indication of its success, LLR achieved an 18% increase in the key indicator of fundraised income on a reduced fundraising cost ratio in the last 12 months.

5 Improving leadership team performance

Having described all the characteristics of leadership teams and how well each component of leadership team work is delivered, we can now go on to develop a complete picture of the performance of leadership teams and to pinpoint the overall drivers of outstanding performance.

In this chapter we look at:

- the overall effectiveness of leadership teams

- the characteristics that drive high performance

- how well participants perform on the drivers

- the prevalence of drivers across all leadership teams

- future priorities to further improve leadership team performance.

5.1 Overall effectiveness of leadership teams

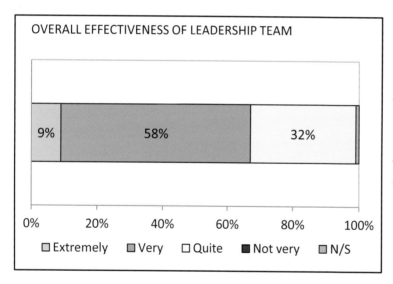

Participants were asked to think about all the topics raised in the questionnaire and rate overall the effectiveness of their leadership team Two thirds (67%) of chief executives rated their leadership team as extremely or very effective and one third reported that their team was only quite effective.

When we looked at their ratings for each of the nine components of effectiveness we saw that chief executives rated their own performance and the size and structure of the team most highly and investment in team development significantly lower than all other components. The ratings given by HR directors were lower by 9% but similarly ranked.

So, with the exception of recruitment and reward, chief executives and HR directors felt that their organisations were better at getting the basic building blocks of the leadership team size, structure and membership in place, but less good at the more demanding activities of leading behaviour, leading strategy and performance, having effective meetings and investing in their own development.

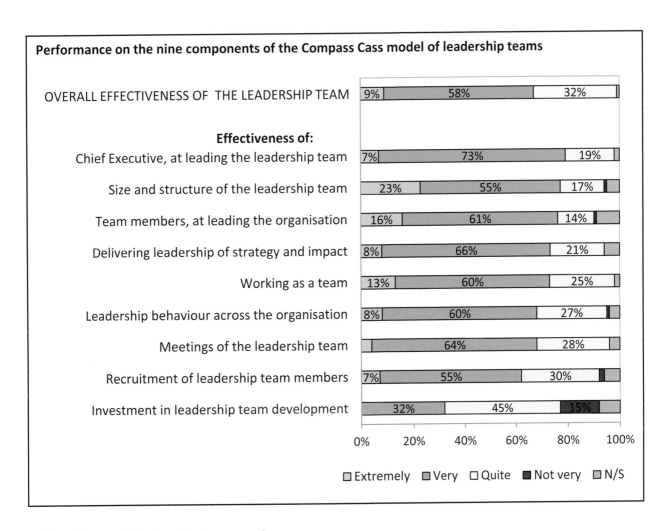

Performance on the nine components of the Compass Cass model of leadership teams

OVERALL EFFECTIVENESS OF THE LEADERSHIP TEAM — 9% | 58% | 32%

Effectiveness of:

Chief Executive, at leading the leadership team — 7% | 73% | 19%

Size and structure of the leadership team — 23% | 55% | 17%

Team members, at leading the organisation — 16% | 61% | 14%

Delivering leadership of strategy and impact — 8% | 66% | 21%

Working as a team — 13% | 60% | 25%

Leadership behaviour across the organisation — 8% | 60% | 27%

Meetings of the leadership team — 64% | 28%

Recruitment of leadership team members — 7% | 55% | 30%

Investment in leadership team development — 32% | 45% | 15%

0% 20% 40% 60% 80% 100%

☐ Extremely ▨ Very ☐ Quite ■ Not very ▨ N/S

5.2 Drivers of leadership team performance

So we know what teams are good and not so good at, but we wanted to shed some light on what drives high performing leadership teams. This will point to the underlying characteristics that deserve greatest attention by leadership teams.

We first looked at the nine components of leadership teams in our model to determine which had most impact in driving up leadership team performance. Whilst correlations do not necessarily imply causation, positive associations may point to characteristics that should be given greater attention in developing team effectiveness.[8]

Whichever way we looked at the data, the three components concerned with the team structure, team membership and recruitment and reward were consistently *less* closely correlated with higher overall team performance. So we concluded that whilst these components around organising the team may be essential building blocks of sound teams, they are not the underlying drivers of outstanding teams.

In contrast, whichever way we looked at the data on the strongest correlations with performance, leadership of behaviour and great team working consistently stood out significantly ahead of the other

---

[8] For more details on the various methods of data analysis employed, see Appendix 5 'Research Methods'

components as correlating with higher performance; these are therefore the topics which contribute most to building outstanding leadership teams. Three further components also emerged from this analysis as being more strongly related to leadership team effectiveness giving five in all that correlated most closely with higher performance. They are in order of importance:

1. Leadership of behaviour across the organisation
2. Great team working
3. Effective team meetings
4. Leadership of strategy and performance
5. Team development. refresh

Relating this back to our original model a picture emerges in which membership, structure, the leader and remuneration can be viewed as the essential building blocks of a strong team, but that outstanding performance is likely to come from focussing on these five 'enabling' components.[9]

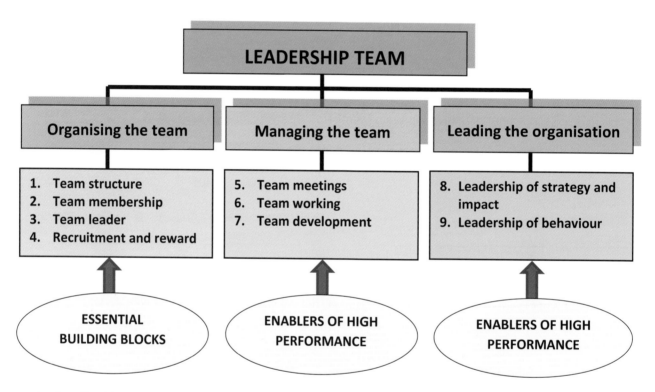

As described in previous chapters, we looked at the underlying characteristics of leadership teams to see which correlated best with the performance of each of the above components of team effectiveness. We did this for each of the nine components in our model.

Drawing together all our analysis we identified the 20 characteristics that are most closely associated with high performing teams. We called them the **drivers** of outstanding leadership team performance. Leadership teams that focus on improving performance in these areas are likely to reap the greatest rewards. None stood out as being a 'magic bullet' but together they point to the characteristics that are

[9] This is consistent with Wageman et al. Harvard Business Review Press who suggest a model of 'essentials' and 'enablers' based on research into corporate sector senior leadership teams in the USA.

most likely to have the greatest leverage on team performance. We used this analysis to develop the our model of outstanding leadership performance.

This identifies the five components of leadership teams that contribute most to effectiveness, with the strongest driver at the top. Below each component we set out the top four characteristics that leadership teams should focus on to deliver that component of team effectiveness.

Together they pinpoint the priorities for all teams that aspire to achieve outstanding performance.

DRIVERS OF OUTSTANDING LEADERSHIP TEAM PERFORMANCE

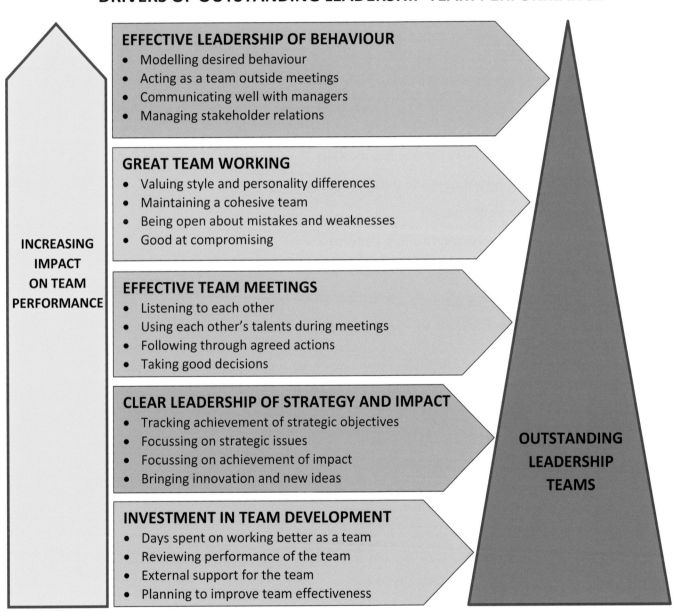

INCREASING IMPACT ON TEAM PERFORMANCE

EFFECTIVE LEADERSHIP OF BEHAVIOUR
- Modelling desired behaviour
- Acting as a team outside meetings
- Communicating well with managers
- Managing stakeholder relations

GREAT TEAM WORKING
- Valuing style and personality differences
- Maintaining a cohesive team
- Being open about mistakes and weaknesses
- Good at compromising

EFFECTIVE TEAM MEETINGS
- Listening to each other
- Using each other's talents during meetings
- Following through agreed actions
- Taking good decisions

CLEAR LEADERSHIP OF STRATEGY AND IMPACT
- Tracking achievement of strategic objectives
- Focussing on strategic issues
- Focussing on achievement of impact
- Bringing innovation and new ideas

INVESTMENT IN TEAM DEVELOPMENT
- Days spent on working better as a team
- Reviewing performance of the team
- External support for the team
- Planning to improve team effectiveness

OUTSTANDING LEADERSHIP TEAMS

5.3   How well leadership teams perform on the drivers

Having pinpointed the 20 drivers of outstanding performance we then mapped how well organisations performed on each of these specific characteristics. They were classified on a two way criterion of 'good' or 'poor' performance.[10]

The table overleaf shows the proportion of organisations that met the criteria for good performance and therefore have the driver in place.

The drivers that we found were most frequently in place were:

- a cohesive team

- with a sharp focus on strategic issues

- that takes good decisions.

We suspect that these are the easier drivers to put in place.

The drivers that were least frequently in place and therefore present the greatest opportunities for improvement were:

- making best use of each other talents during meetings

- innovation and bringing new ideas into the organisation

- plans to improve team effectiveness

- sufficient time spent each year on working better as a team

- utilising external support, including a team coach

- reviewing leadership team performance with input from a range of different stakeholders.

We note that the characteristics with the lowest percentage of organisations reporting good performance are all in the 'team development' heading. We suspect that these are more difficult to implement and should therefore be the focus of attention of teams that have already put the essential components of effective teams in place.

---

[10] The definition of performance varied on each dimension, according to how the characteristic was measured. In most cases it was it was the participant's judgement of how effective their organisation was at performing the particular team role; in a few instances it was the *frequency* of undertaking the activity. For dimensions that were rated on the four point scale, the top two boxes 'extremely' and 'very' were designated as good performance.

How well organisations perform on the 20 drivers of outstanding teams	% of organisations that reported good performance on the driver
EFFECTIVE LEADERSHIP OF BEHAVIOUR	
Modelling the desired behaviours across the organisation	61%
Acting as a team outside of team meetings	60%
Communicating well with managers across the organisation	59%
Systematic at managing relationships with all stakeholder groups	51%
GREAT TEAM WORKING	
Genuinely valuing each other's style and personality differences	52%
A cohesive team	68%
Open about mistakes and weaknesses	63%
Good at compromising	56%
EFFECTIVE TEAM MEETINGS	
Listening to each other in meetings	66%
Using each other's talents well in meetings	50%
Following through on actions after meetings	66%
Taking good decisions	82%
LEADERSHIP OF STRATEGY AND PERFORMANCE	
Tracking the achievement of strategic objectives	58%
Focussing sharply on strategic issues	70%
Focussing on the achievement of impact	65%
Good at innovation and bringing new ideas into the organisation	50%
INVESTMENT IN TEAM DEVELOPMENT	
More than one day spent in the last 12 months specifically on working better as a team	42%
Leadership team performance review, comprising 3 or more review activities	23%
External support for team development, including a team coach	30%
Planning to improve team effectiveness	26%

5.4 *Prevalence of the drivers*

We then looked at how many drivers organisations had in place. On average they had 11 of the 20 drivers of outstanding leadership team performance in place.

We found that 29% of the organisations had 15 or more of the 20 drivers in place – these are the really high performing leadership teams, which have achieved good performance on three quarters of the crucial characteristics.

In contrast, there was a bottom quartile of organisations that had only a third (7 or fewer) of the drivers in place – these

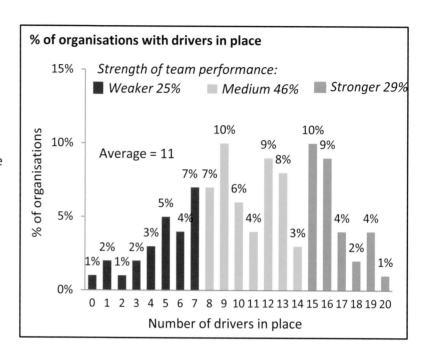

organisations still have much to do in order to improve their leadership team performance.

Chief executives who reported higher overall performance or had more of the drivers of outstanding performance in place were also more likely to believe that their effectiveness had increased over the last two years. This suggests that teams that are committed to improvement do see results.

To complete the picture we investigated *which* charities had 'stronger' leadership teams. The proportion of organisations displaying stronger leadership teams (with 15-20 of the drivers in place) was higher among the following sub-groups:

- charities with higher income (over £50m) and more staff (over 500)

- organisations where the chief executive had a greater breadth of experience

- teams where the chief executive has a long tenure (8 or more years in post)

- teams where are at least half are externally appointed members

- teams where more than two thirds have post graduate qualifications

- teams with a deputy CEO or COO

- ethnically diverse teams.

We also profiled *which* charities had 'weaker' leadership teams. The proportion of organisations displaying weaker leadership teams (with 7 or fewer of the drivers in place) was higher among:

- charities with lower income (less than £20m)

- teams with no (or fewer) people with a postgraduate qualification.

5.5   *Actions across the charity sector*

Finally, we asked chief executives in an open question to think more widely across larger charities and suggest actions that should be taken to improve the performance of leadership teams. Although some of the proposals overlap, in order of most frequently mentioned they recommended:

- paying greater attention to team development including assessing team performance, leadership development programmes, honesty within the team and working on behaviours

- focussing teams more sharply on organisation goals, outcomes and impacts

- stronger individual performance management

- greater use of external support including coaches and mentors

- greater clarity of the roles of the board and management

- having a statement of the organisation's values and living and breathing them.

6 Conclusions

Leadership teams are a critically importing driving force of larger charities. They sit at the apex of organisations and have people with the skills, experience, power and time to have a huge impact on the way organisations work and their overall effectiveness. Leadership teams that work well can ensure organisations are clear about their mission and strategy, have the capacity to deliver them and have a culture that is empowering and motivating for staff, volunteers and the board.

Taking the findings from the literature review, the results of this research along with our experience of working with leadership teams and the input we have received from chief executives and members of leadership teams during this research, we draw the following conclusions:

Drivers of leadership team effectiveness

1. The two strongest drivers of the performance of leadership teams are effective **leadership of behaviour** and **great team working**. These are the topics which talented and stable teams should give the greatest attention to if they wish to build outstanding leadership teams.

2. **Leadership of behaviour** requires leadership team members to model the behaviours they want to see across the whole organisation, be seen to be acting as a team, communicate effectively with managers and nurture all stakeholder relationships systematically. **Great team working** requires that team members genuinely value each other's style and personality differences, work as a cohesive group, are open about mistakes and weaknesses and are good at compromising.

3. The next most important drivers are **effective team meetings, leadership of strategy and impact and investment in team development**.

4. **Effective team meetings** require members to listen to each other and use each other's talents fully in meetings. The highest performing teams are also the practical ones that take good decisions and follow through on agreed actions. **Leadership of strategy and impact** requires teams to be clear about the organisation's strategy, be good at tracking the achievement of strategic objectives and maintaining a sharp focus on strategic issues. **Investment in team development** requires that teams set aside significant time for team development, review honestly their own performance and create plans for improving team performance.

5. These drivers are all easy to state, but **challenging to implement in practice**. In particular, leadership teams can be reticent to be seen to spend significant time and money on themselves, particularly in difficult economic times. Such spending can be particularly difficult to justify when budgets are tight and salary increases for staff are small or non-existent.

Sequencing change

6. Getting the **right people on the team** is a crucial starting point, particularly for new chief executives who can make changes more easily when they are first appointed. Our research suggests they should ideally work towards smaller teams containing some members with post graduate qualifications and then strive to maintain reasonably stable membership.

Investment in team development

7. Our literature review found evidence from management, psychology and financial economics that executive effects on organisational outcomes are both statistically and practically significant. The challenge for chief executives therefore is to demonstrate that any proposed investment in team development **will have a significant impact** on the achievement of their organisations' mission.

8. The boards of larger charities now accept the need for regular and rigorous evaluation of their performance. It is less common for leadership teams to engage in similar evaluations. We conclude that it is equally important for leadership teams to **conduct regular evaluations** of their performance informed by the groups with whom they regularly interact.

9. Chief executives acknowledged that investment in team development was the component in our model of leadership teams where performance was weakest. They also identified it as one of their key future priorities. When they were asked about making improvements across the charity sector, it was the most frequently mentioned action. This suggests that team development should **be given greater attention in future** and tailored carefully to the values and culture of charities and the complexities that their leadership teams have to manage.

10. Teams will always need to re-invest in team development when team members change and the team goes through the well-recognised stages of 'forming, storming, norming and performing'. Investment in **individual development** for the new member(s) is particularly important as they make the large step up from being a manager to becoming a director with a strategic overview of the organisation.

Looking to the future

11. Although leaders can have a more positive view of their performance than their followers, around a third of chief executives felt their leadership teams were **only quite effective**. Furthermore, we discovered that a quarter have seven or fewer of the top 20 drivers in place. We conclude that many larger charities have significant opportunities to improve the performance of their leadership teams.

12. People's behaviour was the strongest driver of outstanding performance in our research into **both governing boards and leadership teams**. Both groups need people who are highly self-aware, able to make robust arguments and understand emotional intelligence and who welcome personal feedback. These characteristics need to be sought when appointing people to board and leadership team positions.

13. The evidence we have gathered has created a solid and reliable overview of the characteristics of leadership teams, which can be **used by leadership teams to benchmark themselves** against similar organisations.

14. As far as we are aware this is the most comprehensive overview of leadership teams that has been created. It provides an opportunity for organisations in the private and public sectors to **learn from the experience of the charity sector**.

7 Implications

There are many implications of this research for chief executives, leadership team members and the other groups that can influence and are affected by the performance of leadership teams. The main implications are:

1. **For chief executives**

   Most chief executives recognise that building an effective leadership team is a critically important activity. They need to:

   a) consider the sequence for making improvements which is likely to involve:

      - getting the right people on the team
      - investing in team development
      - leading behaviour within the team and across the organisation

   b) base any justification for strengthening their leadership teams on more effective achievement of their organisations' missions

   c) work with their leadership teams to identify where their team performs well and to pinpoint areas for improvement

   d) review leadership team performance against the characteristics of effective teams and in particular against the key drivers of outstanding teams

   e) create a plan for continuous strengthening of the leadership team

   f) seek guidance from wise advisors which might include their chairs and board members, peer chief executives, mentors and consultants

   g) ensure that the leadership team discusses its values and acts according to them

   h) integrate communications so manages get a clear and consistent set of messages

   i) allocate responsibilities for managing relationships with each stakeholder group and ensure that stakeholder expectations are met.

2. **For leadership team members**

   Leadership team members can initiate and support actions to strengthen the team. They should:

   a) help to establish a culture of rigorous self-reflection and self-evaluation so all members have a good understanding of their team's strengths and weaknesses

   b) be open and willing to work on making improvements

   c) use surveys of staff opinion to seek views on the performance of the leadership team

   d) use experiences of successful team working as an opportunity to discuss what worked well and why and to embed those behaviours into future working

   e) recognise that they are closely watched by managers who report to them and ensure that leadership team behaviour sets standards of authenticity and openness that they expect to see across the whole organisation.

3. **For board chairs**

    The importance of the leadership team means that chairs should take a particular interest in how well the team is working. Although the final responsibility for decisions on team arrangements, membership and development lies firmly with chief executives, there are some topics that they cannot always discuss with the team itself. Chairs can be a source of independent advice when team leaders face important decisions about the team. They should:

    a) ensure that the performance of leadership teams is a topic for regular reflection and discussion with their chief executives

    b) be aware of the drivers of leadership team effectiveness

    c) assist the chief executive remain true to the values of the organisation

    d) ensure that maintaining an effective leadership team is a formal objective for chief executives and include performance of leadership teams as a topic in annual appraisals

    e) consider making the effectiveness of the leadership team a criteria for pay awards particularly for those chief executives who receive performance related pay.

For board members

Many boards hold part of some board meetings with only the chief executive present. This provides an opportunity to discuss whether the leadership team has the capacity to deliver the organisation's strategy. Good boards can bring wisdom and experience that can help chief executives make the best judgements on strengthening their team.

Board members should:

a) share their reflections on the leadership team in private sessions with the chief executive

b) empower chief executives to make any necessary changes and support them when implementation gets difficult

c) be active contributors to 360° reviews of leadership team performance

d) ensure that there are appropriate budgets for creating and strengthening leadership teams.

For HR directors

HR directors have the skills and experience to be trusted advisors to chief executives. They can:

a) support chief executives who are considering changing or developing their team

b) take responsibility for shaping team performance reviews and managing team development

c) ensure that all changes are tailored to fit the organisation's desired culture and values.

For senior managers

Leadership teams need feedback, and the most pertinent will often come from the managers who report to them. Senior managers should:

a) contribute to formal feedback on leadership team performance

b) be a source of informal feedback, sharing information about how top teams are perceived and what they most need to do to ensure effective delivery of their organisations' missions

Appendix 1   Summary of literature review

"In order to understand why organizations do what they do, or perform the way they do, we need to deeply comprehend the people at the top – their experiences, abilities, values, social connections, aspirations and other human features. The actions – or inactions – of a relatively small number of key people at the apex of an organization can dramatically affect organisational outcomes"
(Finkelstein et al, 2009)

Background

This literature review was conducted to inform the Compass Partnership and Cass Business School research into increasing the effectiveness of senior leadership teams in large UK charities. It helped to shape the model of leadership teams and the questionnaires used to gather our primary data.

Whilst there is a large literature on teams in general, there is very little on leadership teams and virtually nothing specifically on leaderships teams in civil society organisations. This review therefore draws mainly on the limited literature from the for-profit sector most of which comes from the USA.

Any research into the effectiveness of leadership teams raises the challenge of how effectiveness is measured, a problem that is particularly difficult in charities because they don't have a simple financial 'bottom line' to track performance. For the purposes of this research we define effectiveness of the leadership team as **'the *capacity* of its members to work together to maximise the *potential* of their charity to achieve its mission'**.

A key and seminal piece of research in this area is known as Upper Echelons theory (Hambrick & Mason, 1984) which suggests that chief executives do not make strategic choices on their own but that the senior leadership team often bears responsibility for strategic decisions. The authors suggest that executives 'make choices on the basis of their personalized construals of the situations they face' (Hambrick, 2007); that executives differ in their behaviours and choices and organizations become a reflection of their top managers (Finkelstein et al, 2009).   From this work many studies have followed looking at the demographic make-up of the senior team and its impact on organisational performance.

Membership of the leadership team

No studies identified as part of this review appear to specify an optimum size for an effective leadership team although size is a factor in considering performance or functioning (Haleblian & Finkelstein (1993).

A study by Simons, Pelled & Smith (1999) suggests heterogeneous teams (diverse in the dimensions of education, functional background and tenure) that engage in debate are more likely to formulate comprehensive strategies that also lead to higher levels of performance.

Narango-Gill, Hartmann and Mass (2008) report that during periods of strategic change, leadership team heterogeneity appears to have 'a substantial positive effect on operational performance.'

Olson et al (2006) note research that heterogeneous teams will be more creative than homogeneous ones (in demographic terms) and will cast a wider net on information while evaluating various alternatives (Wiersema & Bantel, 1992). O'Reilly, Snyder & Boothe (1993) found that team homogeneity promotes co-operation essential for implementing strategic decisions.

Wageman et al (2008) suggest three essential conditions for leadership team effectiveness namely that:

- the team 'has to be a real team' with clear boundaries as to who is there and why
- there is a clear and compelling purpose for the team to exist
- the importance of having 'the right people on the team and the wrong people off'.

The difference the leadership team can make

Carpenter et al (2004) note that there is cumulative evidence 'from management (Carpenter et al, 2004), psychology (Peterson et al, 2003) and financial economics (Bertrand & Scholar, 2003) that executive effects on organisational outcomes are both statistically and practically significant'.

Edmondson et al (2003) report that both practitioners and scholars have argued that teamwork at the top of an organization promotes creativity, enables executives to utilize diverse experience in problem solving and provides a mechanism to cope with the turbulence and complexity of the external environment.

Leadership behaviours

A number of studies focus on the impact of leadership (chief executive) behaviours on the senior team. Three identified during this review include:
- Carmeli, Schaubroeck & Tishler (2011) who suggest that empowering leadership shapes leadership team behavioural integration and potency, thereby enhancing organisational performance;
- Srivastava, Bartol & Locke (2006) who seek to demonstrate that empowering leadership behaviours (whereby power is shared with subordinates and raises levels of intrinsic motivation) is positively related to both knowledge sharing and team efficacy which in turn are both positively related to performance. Findings indicate that although 'empowering leadership did not have a direct effect on performance, it is likely that its presence leads to higher team efficacy and knowledge sharing both of which are desirable for team effectiveness'
- Stoker, Grutterink and Kolk (2012) who suggest that for high-feedback seeking leadership teams, positive organisational results can be achieved without a transformational team leader.

Research in the nonprofit sector

Frahm & Brown (2007) suggest that the exercise of strategic leadership is different in the nonprofit sector; Taliento & Silverman (2005) identify areas where leaders might need to adapt for-profit sector leadership practice including:
- the need to pay more attention to communication
- the need for innovative performance management metrics.

Bonner (2010) who identified the six most common challenges faced by nonprofit leadership teams:
- Lack of a big picture perspective
- Lack of a shared direction, priorities, goals, and/or values
- Individuals are not held accountable and poor performance is tolerated
- Business acumen and other needed competencies are missing
- Communication and team meetings are ineffective
- Personality and style differences of team members are not valued.

Practitioner literature

Higgs (2006a) highlights the on-going tension between academic (empirical and organisationally based research) and practical application and experience in particular in the field of working with leadership teams. Practitioner literature identified during this review includes:

- Katzenbach (1997) suggesting that leadership teams are not in fact 'real' teams
- Kruyt, Malan & Tuffield (2011) describing three steps to build a better top team:
    - Get the right people on the team and the wrong people off
    - Make sure the top team does only the work it can do
    - Address team dynamics and processes
- Lencioni (2012) offering a model suggesting four disciplines for the leadership team to follow to ensure organisational health:
    - Build a cohesive leadership team
    - Create clarity
    - Over-communicate clarity
    - Re-enforce clarity
- Ward et al (2007) considering the impact of differences in organisational values within a leadership team
- Crutchfield & McLeod Grant (2007) suggesting six practices for high impact in nonprofits including the need for chief executives 'to share power in order to be a stronger force for good. They distribute leadership throughout their organization empowering others to lead'.

Future research into leadership teams in the nonprofit sector

There appears to be ample opportunities for future research into the area of nonprofit leadership teams. Phipps & Burbach's (2010) propositions for research are that effective nonprofit strategic leaders:

1. increase the organisation's learning capacity
2. increase the organisation's capacity for change
3. improve organisational performance through the exercise of managerial wisdom
4. contribute to improved organisational innovation in nonprofits
5. contribute to mission trajectory
6. and that organisational context influences the behaviours of an effective nonprofit strategic leader.

References

Bertrand & Scholar (2003), Managing with style: the effect of managers on firm policies, The Quarterly Journal of Economics, 118 – 4

Bonner L (2010), Building healthy and effective nonprofit leadership teams, Dewey & Kaye consultancy

Carmeli, A., Schaubroeck, J., & Tishler, A. (2011), How CEO Empowering Leadership Shapes Top Management Team Processes: Implications for Firm Performance, The Leadership Quarterly, 22 (2), 399-411

Carpenter M A, Geletkanycz M A, Sanders W G (2004), Upper Echelons Research Revisited: Antecedents, Elements and Consequences of Top Management Team Composition, Journal of Management, Vol 30, 6: 749-778

Crutchfield & McLeod Grant (2007), Forces for Good, The six practices of high-impact nonprofits, Jossey Bass

Edmondson A C, Roberto M A, Watkins M D (2003), A dynamic model of TMT Effectiveness: Managing unstructured task streams, The Leadership Quarterly, 14 No 3: 297-325

Finkelstein, S Hambrick D C & Cannella A A (2009), Strategic Leadership Theory and Research on Executives, Top Management Teams and Boards, New York, NY, Oxford University Press

Frahm J, Brown K (2007), First steps: linking change communication to change receptivity, Journal of Organizational Change Management, 20.3: 370-38

Haleblian J, Finkelstein S (1993), Top Management Team Size, CEO dominance and firm performance: the moderating roles of environment turbulence and discretion, Academy of Management Journal, 36, 4: 844-863

Hambrick D C, Mason D (1984), Upper Echelons: The Organization as a Reflection of its Top Managers, Academy of Management Proceedings, p12-16

Hambrick, D C (2007), Upper Echelons Theory: an update, Academy of Management Review, Vol. 32 Issue 2: 334-343

Higgs M (2006a), How do top teams succeed? Factors that contribute to successful senior management team performance, Journal of General Management, Vol 32. No 2 Winter

Katzenbach J R (1997), The Myth of the Top Management Team, Harvard Business Review, Vol 75 Issue 6: 83-91

Kruyt M, Malan J, Tuffield R (2011), Three Steps to Building a Better Top Team, McKinsey Quarterly Issue, 1:113-117

Lencioni P (2012), The Advantage, Jossey-Bass

Narango-Gil D, Hartmann F and Maas V S (2008), Top management team heterogeneity, strategic change and operational performance, British Journal of Management Vol 19: 222-234

Olson B J, Parayitam S, Twigg N W (2006), Mediating role of strategic choice between Top Management Team diversity and firm performance: Upper Echelons Theory Revisited, Journal of Business and Management, Vol. 12, 2 111-126

O'Reilly III, C. A., Snyder, R. C., & Boothe, J. N. (1993), Effects of executive team demography on organizational change, In G. P. Huber & W. H. Glick: Organizational Change and Redesign: Ideas for Insights for Improving Performance, New York, NY, Oxford University Press

Peterson R S, Brent Smith D, Martorana P V, Owens P D(2003), The impact of Chief Executive officer personality on top management team dynamics, Journal of Applied Psychology, 88, 5: 795-808

Phipps K A, Burbach M E (2010), Strategic Leadership in the Nonprofit Sector: opportunities for research, Journal of Behavioral & Applied Management, Vol. 11 Issue 2: 137-154

Simons T, Pelled L H & Smith K A (1999), Making use of difference: diversity, debate and decision comprehensiveness in top teams, Academy of Management Journal, 42: 662-673

Srivastava A, Bartol K M, Locke E A (2006), Empowering Leadership in Management Teams: Effects on Knowledge Sharing, Efficacy and Performance, Academy of Management Journal, 49, 6: 1239-1251

Stoker J I, Grutterink H, Kolk N J (2012), Do transformational CEOs always make the difference? The role of TMT feedback seeking behaviour, Leadership Quarterly, 23 p582- 592

Taliento L & Silverman L (2005), A corporate executive's short guide to leading nonprofits, Strategy and Leadership, 33: 5-10

Wageman R, Nunes D A, Burrus J A, Hackman J R (2008), Senior Leadership Teams – what it takes to make them great, Harvard Business School Press

Ward A J, Lankau M J, Amason A C, Sonnenfeld J A, Agle B R (2007), Improving the Performance of the Top Management Team, MIT Sloan Management Review, Spring 2007, 3: 85-90

Wiersema, M, Bantel K (1992), Top Management Team demography and corporate strategic change, Academy of Management Journal, Vol 35, 1: 91-121

Appendix 2   Glossary

Term	Definition
Characteristics	The 75 dimensions that attempt to fully explain the performance of leadership teams in large UK charities.
Components	The nine groupings of characteristics in the Compass Cass leadership team model: 1. team membership 2. team structure 3. team leader 4. team recruitment and reward 5. team meetings 6. team working 7. team development 8. leadership of strategy and performance 9. leadership of behaviour across the organisation.
Drivers	The characteristics of leadership teams that our research found have the greatest impact in increasing the effectiveness of leadership teams.
Enablers	The five components of leadership teams that were found to have greater impact in increasing overall effectiveness of leadership teams.
Stakeholders	People or other organisations who have an acknowledged interest in the organisation, including members, funders, purchasers, service users, board and committee members, managers, staff, volunteers and branches.
Average	The arithmetic 'mean' response.
Typical	The 'modal' response (i.e. the most frequently occurring response).

Term	Definition
Leadership team	The group defined in blue below.
Core group	A group of directors (e.g. those based in one location) who might meet more regularly than the full leadership team.
Wider senior team	A group of directors who report to the chief executive but are NOT part of the leadership team.

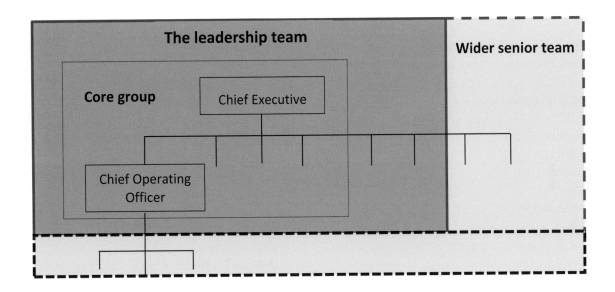

Appendix 3   Participating organisations

Arts and culture organisations
Arts Council of Wales
Culture and Sport Glasgow
Historic Royal Palaces

Colleges and university colleges
Universities and Colleges Admissions Service

Disability organisations
Action on Hearing Loss
Alzheimer Scotland
Diabetes UK
Papworth Trust
Scope
Scottish Autism
Sense
Sense Scotland
Stroke Association
Treloar Trust
United Response

Education and research
Higher Education Academy
James Hutton Institute
John Innes Centre
Leukaemia and Lymphoma Research
National Centre for Social Research
Structural Genomics Consortium

Environment and animal welfare
Donkey Sanctuary
Land Restoration Trust
Milton Keynes Parks Trust
The Conservation Volunteers
Woodland Trust
WWF UK

Funders
ABF The Soldiers Charity
Forces in Mind Trust
Great Ormond Street Hospital Children's Charity

Hospital Saturday Fund
Movember Europe
People's Heath Trust
Royal Navy and Royal Marines Charity
Stewardship
Wellcome Trust

Health provider organisations
CLIC Sargent Cancer Care for Children
Horder Healthcare
Hospital of St John and St Elizabeth
Marie Curie Cancer Care
Royal Hospital for Neuro-disability
Together: Working for Wellbeing

Housing and care providers
Acis Group
Anchor Trust
Cheshire Peaks and Plains Housing Trust
Fremantle Trust
Greensleeves Homes Trust
Knowsley Housing Trust
Methodist Homes
Milestones Trust
Poplar Housing and Regeneration Community
   Association
Shelter
St Mungo Community Housing Association
Vale of Aylesbury Housing Trust
Victory Housing Trust

Intermediary and other bodies
Business in the Community
Electrical Safety Council
In Kind Direct
Scottish Council for Voluntary Organisations
Wales Council for Voluntary Action

International development organisations
Children's Investment Fund Foundation
Disasters Emergency Committee
International HIV/AIDS Alliance
International Rescue Committee UK
Mines Advisory Group
Practical Action
ShelterBox
UNICEF UK
Voluntary Service Overseas
WaterAid
World Vision UK

Leisure and recreation
Edinburgh Leisure
Vision Redbridge Culture and Leisure
YHA (England and Wales)

Professional associations
Royal College of Surgeons of England
Royal Institute of British Architects

Schools
Girls' Day School Trust
Haberdashers' Company
London Diocesan Board for Schools
Stamford Endowed Schools
Woodard Academies Trust

Social welfare providers
Avenues Trust Group
BSS
Children's Society
Crime Reduction Initiatives
Crisis
Friends of the Elderly
Girlguiding
Jewish Care
Making Space
National Childbirth Trust
Norwood
Prince's Trust
Royal National Lifeboat Institution
Samaritans
Scout Association
St John Ambulance
St John of God Hospitaller Services
Turning Point Scotland
Victim Support
West Midlands Special Needs Transport

Training and employment
Engineering Construction Industry Training
 Board

Appendix 4 Profile of participants

Charity size

The total annual income of the 102 charities responding to the survey was £4.7bn representing 17% of the total income of the top 500 (£26.8bn). The threshold for inclusion in the top 500 was an income of £15.8m.

Reflecting the charity sector as a whole, the income of the sample was a skewed distribution with a small number of organisations representing a large proportion of the income. Three quarters of charities had income below £50m. A minority of very large charities, each with income over £100m, made up only 9% of the survey sample yet contributed a third (33%) of its total income.

The majority (77%) of charities employed over 100 staff and a quarter employed over 1,000.

Types of organisation

The top 500 charities were categorised into sixteen types of organisation that reflected the activities that they delivered. The table opposite shows how the survey sample was a reasonably good match by type with arts and culture organisations and religious and spiritual organisations being the only sectors notably under-represented.

Respondent characteristics

91% of participating team leaders had the job title 'Chief Executive'; 4% were the 'Executive Director', 1% were 'Director General', 1% were 'Principal/Vice Chancellor' and 2% had other job titles. Two thirds were men (68%) and one third were women (32%). The average age was 54 but men had a slightly younger age profile:

Age of participating chief executives, by gender	Men (n=69)	Women (n=33)
35-39	1%	-
40-44	7%	9%
45-49	19%	18%
50-54	26%	18%
55-59	22%	27%
60-64	17%	15%
65-69	3%	9%
Not stated	4%	3%
Average	53	54

UK's largest charities, by income and type	Number of charities	% of charities	Number in our sample	% in our sample
Total income:				
Over £100m	56	11.1%	9	8.8%
£50.1m - £100m	82	16.2%	16	15.7%
£25.1m - £50m	176	34.9%	38	37.3%
Under £25m	191	37.8%	39	38.2%
Type:				
Housing and care providers	80	15.8%	13	12.7%
Social welfare providers	77	15.2%	20	19.6%
Arts and culture organisations	49	9.7%	3	2.9%
Education & research organisations (excluding colleges/schools)	42	8.3%	6	5.9%
Disability organisations	39	7.7%	11	10.8%
Aid agencies	36	7.1%	11	10.8%
Environment and animal welfare organisations	30	5.9%	6	5.9%
Funders	29	5.7%	9	8.8%
Health providing organisations	25	5.0%	6	5.9%
Professional associations	17	3.4%	2	2.0%
Leisure and recreation	16	3.2%	3	2.9%
Schools and groups of schools	15	3.0%	5	4.9%
Training, employment and examination providers	15	3.0%	1	1.0%
Colleges and university colleges	14	2.8%	1	1.0%
Religious and spiritual organisations	11	2.2%	0	0.0%
Intermediary and other bodies	10	2.0%	5	4.9%
TOTAL	**505**	**100%**	**102**	**100%**

The organisation types highlighted in green are slightly over represented and those in red are slightly under represented.

Appendix 5   Research methods

We began our research by attempting to identify the most important 'characteristics' of charity leadership teams that need to be in place for an organisation to be well led and managed. We carried out a thorough review of the academic literature and used this along with our experience to produce possible characteristics. We organised these into the research model shown in Appendix 6 and designed a questionnaire which we piloted with experienced chief executives.

After piloting, the resulting postal self-completion questionnaire was sent to chief executives of the top 500 charities (by income) in the UK.[11] The survey was therefore an attempted census of the UK's largest charities. The final questionnaire contained 134 questions, 63 of which asked for facts about the organisation's leadership team arrangements, 63 asked for opinions on a graded scale and 8 were open questions requiring a self-composed response.

After a fieldwork period of nearly 4 months, from October 2013 to January 2014, a total of 102 charities completed the questionnaire giving a response rate of 20%. In a climate of diminishing survey response rates we consider this to be an excellent result from a group of such senior, busy individuals. Feedback from a fifth of the top 500 charities, with a good match between the profile of the top 500 and the 102 participants in terms of both organisation type and size (by income) means we can have reasonable confidence in the validity and broader applicability of the findings.

However, there is a possibility of non-response bias, whereby chief executives have different views from respondents leading to a bias in our findings. In order to test whether chief executives 'over-rated' their leadership team performance, we invited chief executives to nominate their human resources director to complete a parallel questionnaire so that we could corroborate the findings: 18 returned a completed questionnaire. For these 18 participating organisations, we compared their scores and there was close agreement but with HR directors tending to give a marginally lower score than their corresponding chief executives. There were only a few instances of a large disparity of opinion.

This exercise suggested that chief executives' opinions are a reliable surrogate for those of the whole leadership team but are slightly inflated. Ideally we would have invited all team members to complete a questionnaire, for a greater degree of corroboration and perhaps even more broadly to include other stakeholders through 360 degree evaluation of team performance but resources did allow for an exercise on this scale.

The survey results gave us over 11,000 answers to questions about charity leadership. When analysed, this produced 1,800 tables of data to evaluate. The most pertinent evidence is included in the main body of this report.

---

[11] The names of the top 500 were provided by Charities Direct, which up-dates its list quarterly.

In tables and charts throughout this report the sample base for percentaged survey results is 'All 102 participants' unless stated otherwise. All percentages cited in tables are column percentages unless specified otherwise. Percentage responses in tables may not always add up to exactly 100%, due to rounding, or because more than one response was allowed (if more than 100%), or incomplete responses (if less than 100%). All income data cited are per year, unless specified otherwise. When the commentary refers to the 'average' this is the arithmetic mean.

We performed a key driver analysis to deduce which of the many factors we explored had greatest impact on the overall performance of leadership teams. The inherent assumption here is that where associations between variables exist, this suggests a causal link between them (even though causality cannot be proven definitively). The analysis was an iterative process. First we looked at cross tabulations between different variables to see which were more closely associated with higher team performance. Secondly we ran correlations between key variables of interest to look further into the strength of associations.

Because of the small sample base in statistical terms, of just over 100 records, we were cautious about employing multivariate analysis; however we did run a multiple regression analysis to test for predictors of overall team performance and the results were encouraging with the contributing independent variables explaining nearly two thirds of the variance in the dependent variable, overall team effectiveness. In the end we weighed up the results from all three methods and drew conclusions where there was greatest consistency in the findings.

The five components that we identified as drivers in our model were those which consistently showed the strongest associations with the rating of overall leadership team effectiveness. The 20 characteristics we identified within these five components as having most impact were those variables which were most strongly associated with the overall rating on that component. So the driver analysis was performed at two levels: underlying characteristics that had most impact on components, and components which had most impact overall team effectiveness.

Appendix 6   The full research model

LEADERSHIP TEAM

Organising the team

Team Structure
- Organisation design
- Size of team
- Roles on the team
- Geographic location

Team Membership
- Diversity
- Internal/external appointment
- Appointed by current CE
- Tenure

Team Leader
- Demographics
- Previous experience
- Tenure
- Reward
- Delegation skills
- Clarity of member objectives
- Holding team to account
- Admitting mistakes
- Development of member team working skills

Team recruitment and reward
- Selection
- Flexibility of employment
- Performance related pay

Managing the team

Team meetings
- Types
- Frequency
- Duration
- Chairing
- Away days
- Meetings with wider teams
- Agenda management
- Behaviour in meetings
- Decision quality
- Following through actions
- Review of meeting performance

Team working
- Clarity of team purpose
- Collective responsibility
- Passionate debate
- Primacy of organisation interests
- Valuing personality differences
- Cohesiveness
- Emotional intelligence
- Openness and mutual trust
- Openness about mistakes
- Calling behaviour to account
- Ability to compromise

Team development
- Review of team performance
- Plans to improve performance
- One to one meetings
- Member personality types
- Support for team members
- Types of team development
- Time on team development
- Team facilitation
- Team coaching
- CE team leadership skills
- Celebrating success
- Departure from the team

Leading the organisation

Leadership of strategy and performance
- Agreement on objectives
- Quantification of objectives
- Wide understanding of objectives
- Strategic focus
- Innovation
- Responsiveness to change
- Tracking strategic performance
- Tracking operational performance
- Tracking financial performance
- Managing risk
- Focus on impact

Leadership of behaviour
- Expected behaviours
- Establishing team values
- Acting as a team
- Modelling desired behaviour
- Cross organisation working
- Learning culture
- Working with the board
- Chair CE relationship
- Managing stakeholder relationships
- Communicating with managers

Acknowledgements

We are most grateful our colleagues at Compass and Cass Business School and to the chief executives who attended our workshops and those who commented on and tested the draft questionnaire and those who commented on the draft report including:

Adrian Bagg	Papworth Trust (now at MHA)
Julie Bentley	Girlguiding
Alvaro Bermejo	International HIV/AIDS Alliance
David Bilton	Woodard Academies Trust
Henny Braund	Anthony Nolan Trust
Paul Breckell	Action on Hearing Loss
Lorraine Clifton	CLIC Sargent Cancer Care for Children
Sue Delafons	Compass Partnership
David Foster	The Parks Trust
Denise Fellows	Cass Centre for Charity Effectiveness
Barbara Frost	WaterAid
Richard Furze	Friends of the Elderly
Cathy Gilman	Leukaemia and Lymphoma Research
Euan Hall	The Land Trust
Denise Hatton	YMCA England
Richard Hawkes	SCOPE
Beryl Hobson	National Childbirth Trust
Sue Holden	Woodland Trust (now at Earthwatch)
Julie Hopes	The Conservation Volunteers
Robin Jackson	British Academy
Steve James	Avenues Trust Group
Paul Jenkins	Rethink
Catherine Johnstone	Samaritans
Tobias Jung	Cass Centre for Charity Effectiveness
Sue Killen	St John Ambulance
Anne Linsey	YMCA Training
George Levvy	Compass Partnership
Marg Mayne	VSO
Simon Morris	Jewish Care
Paul Palmer	Cass Centre for Charity Effectiveness
Harry Rich	Royal Institute of British Architects
Campbell Robb	Shelter
David Royce	CRI (now independent)
Carole Sawyers	Fremantle Trust
Keith Smith	Compass Partnership

Angus Somerville	The Royal Hospital for Neuro-disability
Jon Sparkes	UNICEF UK
Philip Thicknesse	The Haberdashers' Company
Alison Wallace	ShelterBox
Rachel Westcott	WaterAid
Susan Willoughby	Care South

We are also most grateful to Fiona Ash, Researcher at the Cass Centre for Charity Effectiveness who spent many hours poring over books and articles and writing the review of the literature.

We greatly appreciate the support from Chris Bowden and Colin Slocombe at Marketing Means in managing distribution of questionnaires and data entry, from Andrew Driver for preliminary analysis of all the findings and accommodating our many requests for additional data tables, and from Geoff Inglis for advice on key driver analysis.

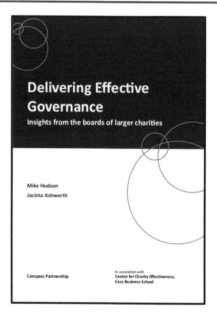

The first investigation by Compass Partnership and Cass Business School looked in detail at the governance of the top 500 charities in the UK and identified the key drivers of governance effectiveness.

Available from DSC via their website or by phone

www.dsc.org.uk/guc

publications@dsc.org.uk

Tel: 0845 077 7707